D1190987

THREE ARGENTINE THINKERS

Three Argentine Thinkers

SOLOMON LIPP

Boston University

PHILOSOPHICAL LIBRARY

New York

Copyright, 1969, by PHILOSOPHICAL LIBRARY, INC.,
15 East 40th Street, New York, N. Y. 10016
ALL RIGHTS RESERVED

Library of Congress Catalog Card No. 68-56191

MANUFACTURED IN THE UNITED STATES OF AMERICA

TO SYLVIA

in homage
and
devotion

TABLE OF CONTENTS

PREFACE

IT IS ONLY in recent years that philosophic thought in Latin America, specifically that of the contemporary period, has begun to filter through to English-speaking circles which concern themselves with intellectual history.

The first landmark in this development was William Rex Crawford's *A Century of Latin American Thought*, a survey and interpretation of the contributions made by representative intellectual luminaries of the Latin American galaxy. This was followed by an excellent English translation of the anthology by Aníbal Sánchez Reulet, *La Filosofía Latinoamericana Contemporánea*. Patrick Romanell's *Making of the Mexican Mind* presented us soon thereafter with a penetrating study of Antonio Caso and José Vasconcelos, as well as contemporary currents in Mexican philosophy. Irma Wilson had earlier given us a comprehensive study of Mexican thought, as this pertained to the educational development of the country. Occasional articles have appeared in journals of philosophy, dealing with Latin American thinkers, e.g., William S. Kilgore's analysis and critique of a phase of Alejandro Korn's thought. More recently, English translations of some of the works of Samuel Ramos, Leopoldo Zea, João Cruz Costa, Francisco Romero and Risieri Frondizi, have made their appearance.*

The present volume is a modest attempt to examine the thought of three of Argentina's outstanding thinkers. Cutting into a cross-section, so to speak, of Argentina's intellectual development, will reveal not only the close affinity

* See, in this connection, Harold E. Davis and Harold A. Durfee, *The Teaching of Philosophy in Universities of the United States,* Pan American Union, Washington, D.C., 1965, Chapter VI.

ix

that existed between each philosopher and the political and cultural environment which he reflected and, in turn, helped to mould, but also the parallel situation that obtained in the philosophic realm of other countries of the Western world, i.e., Argentina was experiencing philosophic movements, similar to those going on elsewhere. In this connection, it should perhaps be pointed out that although Latin American philosophers have no doubt been strongly influenced by European philosophic trends, they have not been blind imitators. They have, rather, selected carefully those elements which they hope will help them in their attempt to analyze and evaluate their own social and cultural milieu.

In order to properly delimit the area to be treated, it was considered feasible to begin with the Positivist era, which greatly stimulated interest on the continent as a whole, coinciding as it did with the economic and industrial expansion of the country. The second act in the drama, namely, the reaction against Positivism, may well be thought of as a transition that led to the third and final stage, i.e., the contemporary period.

Each of these intervals is personified by a philosopher whose works have here been examined. They represent, perhaps better than anyone else, the pulse and temper of their respective philosophic milieux, beginning with Positivism and naturalism (Ingenieros), then proceeding to the inevitable reaction against a rigid determinism, a reaction characterized by an emphasis on human freedom within a framework that may be designated as personalism (Korn), and finally, ending with a most comprehensive system of transcendentalist anthropology (Romero).

The author expresses his fervent hope that in the not too distant future, scholars in the field may be sufficiently motivated to further acquaint the English-speaking public with works of the many philosophers, not only of contemporary Argentina, but also of other countries of the Latin American continent.

This study was made possible by a United States Fulbright research grant in 1963, in addition to a partial grant awarded by the Social Science Research Council. Assistance for clerical help was also afforded by the Graduate School of Boston University. To all of these, the author expresses his indebtedness as well as his profound gratitude. Finally, a special word of thanks is hereby extended to Juan Carlos Torchia-Estrada, of the Pan American Union, Washington, D.C., for his helpful comments and suggestions.

S. L.

CHAPTER ONE

The Historical Setting

IN ORDER TO evaluate critically the particular characteristics of Positivism, as this evolved in Argentina, it is essential to examine the movement as a whole. A brief consideration of the history of Positivist tendencies in Latin America should provide the necessary background and perspective which will enable us to appreciate the various nuances of the movement, the similarities and differences as these developed on the Argentine scene, in contrast to those on the continent in general.

What was the genesis of the movement? Was it a reaction to something? If so, what? How was it received? What, in general, can be said of the philosophic picture of Latin America as a whole?

The early decades of the colonial period in the New World were characterized by the domination of Scholastic philosophy, employed as the "handmaiden" to fortify a theological-political *Weltanschauung* fostered by the mother country. Philosophy was no mere intellectual exercise; it was utilized to justify the structure of a new and powerful empire, an empire that was to insure its perpetuation by resisting any potentially dangerous ideological currents.

Theology was not the exclusive domain of Spain. Europe in general was concerned with theological matters. However it was in Spain, due to a series of historical and ethnic factors, that this concern had assumed exaggerated proportions —so much so, that no price was too high to pay to achieve what went under the name of national and religious unity.

The New World offered fertile soil for further conquest, conquest for the glory of the State as a political force and for the Church as a religious influence. The mother country had determined to close its doors to the "Lutheran heresy" and to the rebellious spirit in general, characteristic of the Renaissance. It utilized Scholastic philosophy to achieve its ends.

Scholasticism, brought to the New World by the religious orders, represented the formula, indeed the entire defensive armor to be utilized for the purpose of keeping the colonies from succumbing to undesirable influences. In short, while Europe was making its way from the Renaissance toward what was eventually to lead to Descartes and experimental science, Spain was returning to medieval philosophy in the form of St. Thomas Aquinas.

True, there was a brief moment of Renaissance humanism which was allowed to break through prior to the Council of Trent. The influence of Erasmus was felt not only in Spain but in the colonies as well. The works of Fray Juan de Zumárraga, one of the founders of the University of Mexico and an enthusiastic admirer of Erasmus, were allowed to circulate.[1] Juan Luis Vives also had his disciples in the New World, e.g. Francisco Cervantes de Salazar and Hernán Pérez de Oliva.[2] These, like the master, sought to harmonize the Aristotelian-Christian tradition with the new critical currents.

Spain took from the Renaissance the elements necessary to strengthen the Counter Reformation. The religious orders, upon arriving in the New World, set about immediately to shape the instrumentality with which to propagate the ideology of the mother country.

Although orthodox Aristotelian-Thomistic philosophy predominated, there were sharp differences of opinion between the Jesuits and the Dominicans during the major portion of the 16th century. Universities in Spanish America adhered to orthodox Thomism, thanks to the efforts of the Augustinian and Dominican orders. On the other hand, the Franciscans came under the influence of Duns Scotus. In any case, the 16th century, a period of propulsion and militancy, was replaced in the following century by a spirit of inertia.

Cultural life prospered during the colonial period, but according to at least one critic it was prolific without being productive. "The dual political-clerical absolutism hemmed in the culture . . . within rigid moulds of obedience and tribute."[3] It was a culture rich, not in spirit, but in letter only. It lacked creative ability because it was deluged by rules and ordinances rigidly enforced. However, its sumptuousness cannot be denied. For example, in Lima alone 180 handsomely salaried professors arrived from Spain to teach 2,000 students.[4]

It was the Spanish Father Gerónimo Feijóo (1676-1764), a temperate Cartesian, who was best known as the philosopher of transition. Religiously orthodox, but philosophically eclectic, Feijóo greatly popularized the ideas of Bacon, Newton and the Encyclopedists in Spanish America.

At no definite point can one say with assurance that Scholasticism ended and the experimental era began. It is of interest to note that for a whole century a kind of doctrine of double truth was in existence at the universities of Mexico and Lima. Once the students had begun to work with the experimental method, they were obliged to reduce their *a priori* material to a minimum. Like Feijóo, they recognized reason and experience as the only valid criteria for all matters not directly pertaining to religion and dogma.

However, Scholasticism continued to resist strenuously. As late as 1771 the model University of Salamanca declared that it would not abandon Aristotelian doctrine as applied to theology, since it was that doctrine which more than any other conformed to the religious beliefs of the nation. Those who set the tone of the University were still saying, when asked to modernize the curriculum: "Newton's principles, although they may prepare the student to be a perfect mathematician, do nothing to make him a good logician or metaphysician. (The principles of) Gassendi and Descartes

3

do not represent the revealed truths as much as do those of Aristotle."[5]

Curiously enough, in that same year (1771), the governing clergy of the cathedral of Buenos Aires proposed that teachers of philosophy not be obliged to follow a definite, pre-determined system, especially in physics, that they could replace Aristotle with Newton if such was their desire, and that ultimately they could explain natural phenomena in the light of their observations and experiences of the senses.[6]

This fact sheds an interesting light upon the attempts on the part of daring intellectual spirits to strike out for themselves and receive ideas from abroad with or without the mother country's approval. The spirit of curiosity and investigation would not be downed. One suspects that even government officials and members of the clergy secretly partook of the literary and philosophical fruits forbidden by a mass of ordinances. For example, when Bishop Azanor of Buenos Aires died in 1796, an inventory of his books revealed the works of Milton, Voltaire, Rousseau, Montesquieu and others.[7]

The law prohibiting the entry of certain books seems to have been winked at more often than not. For example, Manuel Belgrano was authorized by the Papal office to translate Rousseau, Montesquieu and Voltaire. The Peruvian, Pablo Olavide, popularized the ideas of Voltaire, Diderot and Rousseau, although subsequently he was to lose his faith in Encyclopedism.[8]

Gregorio Funes, Rector of the University of Córdoba, Argentina, who in his sixties joined the revolutionary movement in 1810, was inspired by Feijóo in the formulation of a course of study for the University. Like Feijóo, he was moderate and cautious, one who preferred to occupy a position midway between Scholasticism and the modern spirit. And just as that great Spanish humanist, Juan Luis Vives, had done almost three centuries before him, he criticized the exaggerated forms of idle disputation, characteristic of the decadent period of Scholasticism.

Thus, intellectual life in the colonies was not all shadow.

John Tate Lanning has adduced evidence to the effect that Descartes, Leibnitz and Newton were taught in the colonial universities. The cultural scene of Hispanic America, asserts Lanning, should be compared with that of Europe. For if, he asks, France was three hundred years ahead of Hispanic America, why then was Voltaire "asking France to crush the infamous 'vestiges of the old'?"[9]

Diffie would seem to disagree with Lanning, asserting that at least in the case of Ecuador, where Copernican theories were alleged to have been taught, "there is little evidence to show that they exerted any influence, and much to demonstrate that Ecuador continued in the Scholastic tradition to the end of the colonial period and even later."[10]

Additional examples can be adduced to illustrate the urge to break with the old. The Peruvian, Pedro Peralta Barnuevo (1663-1743) "corresponded with Feijóo as well as with the French Academy of Sciences."[11] Juan de Soto, a professor in the University of San Marcos, having surveyed the systems of Descartes and Gassendi, decided to accept some of Newton's principles.[12] The great Peruvian scientist, Eusebio Llano Zapata, "attacked the out-moded 'scholastic rigmarole'" and asked his colleagues to abandon Aristotelian concepts which he claimed were "'magician's tricks'" used to "'deceive boobies and seduce the unwary'."[13] The Viceroy Amat of Lima wanted at least one modern philosopher to be taught, and asked that students be permitted to accept any system of philosophy.[14] Another Viceroy, the Archbishop Caballero y Góngora, in 1789, remarked in regard to the new university at Bogotá: "'. . . the object of the plan should be directed to substituting the useful exact sciences for those merely speculative, in which up to now, time has most regrettably been lost'."[15] José Baquíjano, the idol of American liberals, remembering the glorious tradition of the Indian rebellion, led by Tupac Amaru, protested against the miserable conditions of the natives. He spoke out against benevolent despotism, for "'to better man against his will has ever been the deceitful pretext of tyranny'."[16]

In addition, learned enlightened societies were allowed

5

to form. Interest was shown in Benjamin Franklin's experiments in electricity, and Priestley's and Lavoisier's work on the composition of air. The German savant, Humboldt, referred to José Mutis and José Alzate, as being the two greatest scholars in America. Furthermore, in his opinion the enthusiasm shown in Mexico for the study of the exact sciences could not be rivalled by the Old World universities.[17]

But in spite of these welcome signs there were still disquieting ones. As late as 1812, when the Revolution against Spain was in full swing, the clergy interpreted a terrible earthquake that took place in Venezuela " 'as a divine judgment upon the godless revolutionaries'."[18] When asked by the revolutionary government to tell the people that an earthquake is a natural phenomenon, rather than a punishment from heaven, the Archbishop refused to comply and was expelled from the country.

There were still academicians who, in the 19th century, insisted that the sky is a great solid canopy, and that the planets pass through its portholes.[19] Old systems of thought and habituation die hard. The old colonial dikes were still holding up; efforts were continually made, frantically so, to keep them up. Waves of reaction to the onward march of the French Revolution set in and expressed themselves in the Spanish-speaking world on both sides of the Atlantic. In Spain, for example, says Wilson,[20] the church officials turned their attention to protecting their institutions from the ravages of the liberal movement. An archbishop warned his parishioners that an avalanche of Atheism, Materialism, Deism, anti-Monarchism, and anti-Papism, was threatening to destroy all religion. In Peru, Professor Francisco de Arresse harshly criticized the doctrine of the "Social Contract" and denied the right of sovereignty to the people. The system of social contract enunciated by the authors of modern revolutions, claimed Arresse, had drenched the earth in blood.[21]

As the 18th century drew to a close, academic and philosophic discontent merged with political and economic rebellion. The revolutionary period was to last fifteen years.

Relative stability was to continue being postponed for at least fifty years more. When independence was finally achieved, tragedy still faced all of the countries involved: the tragedy of discovering that while republican ideals had been followed, there was no one capable of governing in that spirit. The spirit had not been given an opportunity to develop.

Grim reality opposed idealistic theory. The economic and administrative organization had not been changed by Independence. It seemed that the people had merely exchanged one set of masters for another. A small educated minority was faced with a mass of illiterates. The two groups did not understand each other. The result was anarchy, political and social turmoil, and eventual dictatorship. The ruling class knew only how to command; it did not know what it meant to be defeated at the polls because there had never been any polls.

✔ ✔ ✔

The period immediately following independence was characterized by continual political chaos. Caudillos arose to put a forceful end to anarchy only to be replaced violently by their opponents or rivals.

In this historical setting it should not come as a surprise to discover that not only business and industry but also the arts, sciences and philosophy gravitated toward the political sphere. Philosophy, especially, was political in its orientation. Political thinkers combined whatever philosophical reflections they might have entertained with their vitriolic proclamations which they hurled against the dictator. In this period especially, it was difficult to keep apart philosophy, literature and politics.

Argentina in the colonial period could not help but be influenced by the same currents and cross currents that buffeted the whole of Spanish America. The colonies of the River Plate were not immune to the stern rigorous policies of the mother country, ruled by the Hapsburg dynasty.

The transfer of the Spanish throne in the 18th century from the Hapsburgs to the Bourbons brought about a reaction against intellectual orthodoxy. Liberal currents challenged older, authoritarian traditions. This confrontation of forces, although clothed in different garb at various intervals, was to continue in the decades to come and was also to have its repercussions on the Argentine scene.

The day after Independence was won, Argentina as well as the other new republics discovered that although political emancipation had been achieved, old colonial habits remained, chief among which was the principle of authority, especially powerful in the realm of religion and philosophy.

The problem, then, became one of separating religion from philosophy, a task which had been begun in the middle of the 18th century. The principle of authority was not valid in the realm of philosophy. Authority might be acceptable in religion which was consigned to the divine world. Philosophy, however, dealt with human affairs.

Experience was to be the guiding light, experience which has its origin in the senses and which, as a result, leads to the formation of ideas. This philosophical current obviously stemming from Condillac, Cabanis and Destutt de Tracy, had its spokesmen in Juan Crisóstomo Lafinur, Juan Manuel Fernández de Agüero, and Diego Alcorta. Lafinur and Agüero leaned rather heavily upon the texts of Destutt and Cabanis, respectively, as is shown by Torchia-Estrada in an interesting comparative table.[22]

The French Enlightenment had greatly influenced the revolutionary élite of 1810. The doctrines of Condillac, Destutt de Tracy and Cabanis, known as the "Ideology," were derived from the Enlightenment. The "Ideology" was an attempt to synthesize French rationalism and English empiricism. The Argentine adherents of the "Ideology" possessed unbounded faith in the power of reason which would solve all problems. Optimists that they were, they evidenced a tendency toward universalism. It was here that they ran into serious opposition on the part of those who were more traditional-minded, and who placed greater weight on the particular local customs and historical peculiarities of the land and people.

8

Geographical factors tended to reinforce the differences in ideology on the continent as a whole and in Argentina in particular. The liberal element of the population was usually concentrated in the metropolitan centers or port cities such as Buenos Aires. Commerce implied not only the importation of products from other countries but also contacts with foreign influences. The constellation of more traditionalist and conservative thought was concentrated in the more isolated regions of the country, in the provinces of the "hinterland."

One could also establish a rather high degree of correlation between attitudes and socio-economic status. Liberal and "universalist" or cosmopolitan thinking was generally restricted to the upper classes, the better educated group. On the other hand, the lower, less educated classes tended to adhere to "nativist," "criollo" values. This is essentially what Romero refers to when he speaks of the "universalist mentality," characteristic of an élite which had been in intimate contact with European thought.[23]

Buenos Aires, the port city, became the focal point of concentration for the "Europeanizers," the *Unitarios,* who wanted the province of Buenos Aires to become the leader of a strong centralized government. The resistance to this tendency came from the interior, from the "backward" provinces which insisted upon local autonomy, and which therefore advocated a "federal" organization. The result was civil strife, highlighted for a period of some twenty years by the ruthless dictatorship of Juan Manuel Rosas.

As Argentina struggled to find itself, new philosophic currents were arriving from abroad, competing with one another in an attempt to achieve a position of dominance. Faith in reason had apparently not worked. It did not fit Argentine reality. Revolution, followed by enlightened despotism, liberty without adequate education, anarchy succeeded by tyranny, a desire to break with Spanish tradition (more easily said than done) and become a spiritual copy of France—such was the framework within which the new philosophical influences operated.

9

Perhaps the Encyclopedist élite did not have faith in the ability of the people to react "rationally." The masses were possibly incapable of being swayed by new ideas based on Reason. The nation was more deeply moved, more effectively influenced and dominated by emotions than by reason. Hence, the principal reaction to the disillusionment brought about by French Rationalism appeared in the form of Romanticism which reached the shores of the New World through French, German and English sources.

In Romanticism, the Argentines found an antidote to the disappointing rationalism of an earlier generation. This time they were inspired by a new movement to speak in terms of a "national" consciousness, replete with traditions, autochthonous characteristics, local customs—in short, a "destiny."

The "mystique" of Romanticism was Janus-like in its Utopianism; one face looked back nostalgically toward an idealization of medievalism, while the other faced the future with strong socialist overtones, a socialism which was Saint-Simonian rather than Marxian.

The Romantic upheaval in Argentina coincided with the dictatorship of Juan Manuel Rosas, and resulted in one of the most productive periods of the intellectual history of the nation. This was the moment during which those of Romantic inspiration merged their vision of a more perfect social organization with militant opposition to the Rosas regime. Their convictions moved them to compassion for "the weak, the neglected and the disinherited" for whom the government in power represented only oppression and exploitation.[24]

At this historical juncture, even though Romanticism seemed to be asserting an overpowering influence, the maelstrom of philosophic thought, characteristic of the first half of the 19th century, appeared to embody within itself a stream of oft-contradictory tendencies: French traditionalism (Maistre, Chateaubriand), Cousin's spiritual eclecticism, Bentham's utilitarianism, the Scottish school of "common sense," as well as the romantic and utopian socialism of Fourier and Saint-Simon—all of these vied for attention and were eventually to prepare the philosophical terrain for the advent of Positivism.[25]

❡ ❡ ❡

Since Positivism, as this developed in Argentina, constitutes the very foundation as well as the point of departure for the three Argentine thinkers dealt with in this study, it becomes necessary to examine the nature of this movement, to distinguish its trajectory from that of other Latin American countries, and to look into and evaluate the contributions to Argentine thought made not only by possible precursors, but also by its outstanding spokesmen.

At no stage can it be said that any one given philosophical orientation exercised an overwhelming influence, to the exclusion of other intellectual currents. For example, Scholasticism continued to engage in what may be called a "rear-guard" action for an entire decade after Independence had been won. It has already been pointed out that the Romantic upheaval did not take place in an undisputed manner. Furthermore, many thinkers themselves cut their intellectual teeth in one school only to evolve and "graduate" into another. Alberdi, e.g., began in the Romantic tradition, but ended up in what has been called an "autochthonous Positivism."[26] Generally credited with writing in a strongly Positivistic and "pragmatic" vein, he had his philosophical initiation in the midst of a rather diverse array of talent which included such names as Condillac, Locke, Cabanis, Holbach, Bentham, Rousseau, as well as Echeverría, Cousin and Chateaubriand.[27] Moreover, Catholic thought existed side by side with strongly anticlerical ideology. There were important thinkers who adhered to the traditional Catholicism of the Spanish philosopher, Jaime Balmes.

❡ ❡ ❡

It would seem at the outset that the term "Positivism" itself needs defining. It has to be placed in a definite historical setting. In its strictest sense, of course, it embraces the doctrine outlined by Auguste Comte. If we were to take Comte as a starting point, we would say that Positivism is the doctrine which maintains that only that knowledge is valid which has been arrived at by way of experimental science, in contrast to the opinions held by theologians and metaphysicians.

Kant, after analyzing the contributions of rationalism and empiricism, had arrived at the conclusion that it was impossible to really know the essence of things. Positivism arose as a movement opposed to post-Kantian idealism. This is one aspect of its *raison d'être*. The other phase is characterized by its negative reaction to speculative theism.[28]

Positivism brought with it a theory of knowledge based only upon the reality of facts and on relationships between these facts. It distrusted metaphysics and sought to exclude all *a priori* premises from its theoretical structures. Consistent with this position, it stressed the relative nature of all phenomena, i.e. relative to our position and situation. Ideas are social products and are conditioned by collective organization; they function not only in accordance with individual needs and preferences. Positivism manifested a strong affinity for the "scientific" approach; small wonder it was received joyfully by the scientists of the New World.

The early 19th century ideological cycle in Argentina can be said to have served as a basis for the subsequent infiltration of Positivistic currents. With its emphasis on the naturalistic and anthropocentric orientation, it proved most congenial to the new political and intellectual environment within which the new liberal and democratic state was to grow.

The term "positive" became equated with what is real, natural and objective. In the socio-political sphere it acquired "progressive" implications. Social progress had no need of the "metaphysical."

There were, of course, reverberations of Cousin's eclecticism which tended to act as a counterweight to the liberal-democratic currents in the socio-political field, and the empirical and naturalist tendencies in the philosophical realm. The political evils of the period were attributed to the predominance of secular thinking. Eclecticism, in a sense, prepared the way for a resurgence of Catholicism in the second half of the 19th century. Positivism, a reaction to this resurgence, was an attempt to recapture the naturalist tradition of the Argentine "Ideology" and the progressive democratic tradition of the May Revolution.[29] Moreover, the upsurge of Positivistic and scientific thinking coincided with the accelerated political and cultural development, characteristic of the period of economic expansion, European immigration and national unification.

One must bear in mind, too, that Positivism in Argentina, in contrast to the movement in other Latin American countries, was closely allied with and conditioned by the experimental sciences. Since the scientific approach, strongly polemical in nature, colored the philosophical thinking of the period, i.e. the latter half of the 19th century, it was inevitable that Positivism, too, should find itself arrayed against all transcendentalist currents which were themselves intimately linked with political and social conservatism.[30]

In the case of Argentina, specifically, there has been considerable difference of opinion as concerns the nature and variety of Positivist thinking. It therefore becomes essential at this point to present the differences in emphasis and interpretation. Not only must one distinguish between the Comtian and the later Spencerian variety, as these influenced the Argentine scene; one must also be careful to keep separate the different phases of Comtism itself.

The apparent merging of "scientism" and Positivism, as well as the materialistic overtones associated with evolutionism, utilized by certain Argentine Positivists, has given rise to a series of penetrating questions, posed critically by Perelstein, who complains that the definition and scope of Argentine Positivism has not been brought out with sufficient clarity.[31] Nor is it clear, she affirms, whether those who criticize Argentine Positivism are referring to the Comtian or the Spencerian variety.

To further compound the difficulty, one may ask which phase of the Comtian variety is being referred to, since it is well known that Comte himself is to be studied in two phases: the scientific and the religious. The first stage, the scientific, was an attempt to counteract the social chaos that pervaded France in the 1840's and to introduce a system of order via a knowledge and application of society's laws. Sociology was the capstone which crowned the hierarchy of Comte's classification of the sciences, a hierarchy beginning at the bottom with mathematics, then proceeding to astronomy, physics, chemistry, biology, in that order, and finally sociology. Sociology from on high would insure political order "in the midst of profound moral disorder."[32]

Whereas in 1844 Comte had divorced morality from theology, in the second phase of his writings[33] a decade later, he was gradually evolving toward a new, universal religion of which he considered himself the founder. Religion for Comte had undergone a metamorphosis: he now substituted religion for the science of his earlier period and transformed knowledge and wisdom into faith.

Perhaps the cordial reception accorded to Positivism by Hispanic American intellectuals can best be explained by the opposition, by and large, on the part of the traditional Church to the new states, coupled with the necessity of these states to wrestle with their new environment in an attempt to master it. For in spite of French, German and English influences, the hold which Roman Catholicism continued to exert proved extraordinary. It was primarily to combat the domination of the Catholic Church, that Positivism was made use of to such a great extent. Hispanic American thinkers sought to destroy the prevailing theological and metaphysical theories, and resorted to Comte and Spencer as their intellectual arsenal. It must therefore be remembered that Positivism did not only apply to philosophy, but also to political theory, law, sociology and education. Moreover, Positivism was considered an instrument in a bitter ideological battle and, therefore, had to be polemical in nature. It acquired all the earmarks of a powerful cult, with its Sanhedrin and its priests. People now began to swear by Comte and Spencer, rather than by Francisco Suárez or Saint Thomas.[34]

When man is insecure in his day-to-day existence, when he has serious problems of a social and economic nature to cope with, he is not inclined to indulge in what he considers idle speculation or philosophic web-weaving. He is interested, instead, in the tangible, the scientific (conceived of somewhat narrowly), the operational. It is consequently of interest to note that the wildfire spread of Positivism was the answer to a definite need. In the first place, supported as it was by the prestige of the natural sciences, it was easily grasped not only by scholars, but by the layman. Secondly, when Catholic scholars failed to bring their concepts up to date, to adjust them to the latest scientific discoveries and, consequently, to give satisfactory answers to questions which people were asking, it was inevitable that Positivism would gain masses of adherents. Philosophy was no longer the jealously guarded possession of a select few who hibernated in their secluded retreats. Positivism brought philosophy out into the street for an airing, so to speak.[34a] The examination of philosophical questions was no longer anyone's particular monopoly.

In addition, there was the political factor. Catholicism stood staunchly behind the old ruling families, the well-born, the land-owners and cattle ranchers, who governed with an iron hand. But changes were taking place. The economy was not standing still. New social and economic alignments were shaping up: new groups were in ferment, desirous of sharing political and economic power. Finding their way blocked by vested interests, they quite naturally sought to identify themselves with any movement which challenged the ideological conceptions shared by the aristocracy. Hence the acceleration of anti-clerical feeling, the result of an identification of that feeling with antipathy toward the ruling class. Hence, too, the triumphant onrush of Positivism.

Positivism, then, signalized the end of an era: the esoteric era. Philosophy donned the layman's clothes and was appealed to as a guide to daily behavior, for the solution of problems of the moment. In this sense, Positivism may be viewed as having played a liberating role.[35]

Leopoldo Zea, in his discussion of Positivism in Latin America, makes the interesting point that Positivist philosophy was utilized in various countries for different purposes. Moreover, the reception of Comte's doctrines varied considerably. For, whereas in Brazil e.g., the religious phase of Comte took hold and was diffused throughout the country, in Argentina, by contrast, it was the first phase, the scientific, that predominated. Although the religious views influenced the thinking of some Argentine positivists, they were not institutionalized, as was the case in Brazil.

Generally speaking, positivist thought was viewed in Spanish America as a doctrine of combat, of struggle, and as a means of constructive building of a new order after having broken violently with the old. The Mexicans, e.g., intended to use Positivism as a means of putting an end to the perpetual chaos in which they found themselves. In Argentina it was a weapon to be used to "civilize," i.e., "North Americanize" the country and counteract the influence of the "barbarian" masses who supported the Rosas regime. The Chileans considered Positivism as the road to liberalism. In Uruguay it was a way of putting an end to corruption and military coups. Finally, in Cuba it furnished the theological justification for independence from Spain.[36]

Positivism in Latin America, then, was to be utilized to end internal conflict and to build a new order. For let it not be forgotten that Comte's primary aim was to reorganize society. He believed that the failure of the French Revolution was due to the individualistic Encyclopedists. Such concepts as liberty and the free and unfettered examination of ideas had led to anarchy of thought and behavior. In order, therefore, to achieve unity of thinking it was essential to establish a hierarchical classification of thought—the essence of Comtism.

The uses to which Positivism was put offers an interesting illustration of the intimate connection between philosophical and sociological thought on the one hand, and the reigning political and economic doctrines on the other. As Zea has pointed out,[37] different varieties of Positivism dominated a given situation in accordance with the socio-cultural factors which happened to exercise a commanding position at the moment. For example, the Positivism of Comte subordinated the interests of the individual to those of society. This may be in keeping with the desire of a powerful social group which makes every effort to maintain its position of dominance and control. This group therefore will speak in the name of "society" and will stress "order."

However, a new and ambitious socio-economic group may struggle to achieve power in its desire to win for itself a "place in the sun." In the process of so doing, it clashes with the older group in the economic hierarchy which has exercised this dominance for a longer period of time. The new group, then, will no longer find it profitable to stress "order." It may prefer to emphasize the component element known as "progress." It may, in fact, prefer Spencer to Comte, since English Positivism laid greater stress upon the freedom of the individual to enrich himself, rather than upon harmony as the all-important factor. Or it may be that the *very same* group will be asking for "order" at one moment (and will quell "disturbances" in order to achieve this "harmony") and may, on some subsequent occasion demand "freedom" in the name of "progress," again for the sake of its own interests. Karl Mannheim would seem to give substantiation to this line of thinking: ". . . in the past, as well as in the present, the dominant modes of thought are supplanted by new categories when the social basis of the group of which these thought-forms are characteristic, disintegrates or is transformed under the impact of social change."[38]

In short, the terms "order" and "progress" which constitute the key note of Positivism did not necessarily have to go hand in hand; very often they ran counter to each other. Each factor of the equation was emphasized at a different historical moment to suit the occasion. This is the story of Positivism not only in Argentina, but in Latin America as a whole.

Spencer's individualism, e.g., seemed more attuned to

the era of Argentina's industrial development than Comte's "statism" or "structuralism," although representatives of both tendencies were active. The doctrine of the survival of the fittest was made to serve business interests, conducted by the Argentine bourgeoisie. Spencerian liberalism provided the necessary rationale for individual enterprise—reminiscent of Mexico's "científicos" under the Díaz regime.[38a] The so called "oligarchy" intended to transform the country's economy, "but from above, without permitting the immigrant avalanche to snatch power from patrician hands."[39] Enlightened self-interest, as understood and dictated by utilitarian theory, had joined forces with the doctrine of evolution. As Zea points out, the Argentine bourgeoisie as well as that of other Hispanic American countries found in the doctrines of Spencer and Darwin "the best theoretical justification of their interests..."[40]

Currents of thought do not function in a vacuum. They operate in a culture which is characterized by power relationships and by stress and strain of different social groups. A given philosophy can therefore be made to appear static or dynamic, conservative or progressive, depending upon the social frame of reference within which it is cast.

Max Scheler, e.g., has pointed out that a class which rules society tends to look toward a static philosophy, or at least to emphasize the static elements within a given philosophy in order to maintain the *status quo*. On the other hand, a social class or group without power, one which seeks to better itself, tends to stress dynamic elements of thinking. This would mean that any philosophy could be made to serve the most virtuous, as well as the most nefarious of purposes. "Ebenso verständlich scheint es mir dass die Unterklassen stets zur Werdensbetrachtung, die Oberklassen zur Seinbetrachtung neigen."[41]

✓   ✓   ✓

One should not lose sight of the point of view espoused by Alejandro Korn—not unanimous by any means—which speaks in terms of an "autochthonous" Argentine Positivism, independent of the European brand, whose chief spokesmen were Juan Bautista Alberdi and Domingo Faustino Sarmiento. The point is that the so-called "scientific," European-inspired Positivism of the 1880's must be distinguished from the "native" social Positivism of the earlier Romantic period. The latter had its roots in socio-political, rather than scientific conditions.

The period following Caseros* was characterized by economic progress. Europe had heeded Alberdi's call, and immigrants, chiefly Italian and Spanish, flocked to the Argentine Pampas or scattered in the cities. Indian warfare was a thing of the past. A network of railroads penetrated the hinterland, grain production increased, the cattle industry expanded, schools were built. The emphasis was on the practical, the positive. After Rosas' exile, the members of the opposition returned home to participate in the creation of a new Argentine nation. The country was to be modernized and "civilized." Both Alberdi and Sarmiento looked to "Europeanization" as the cure for the nation's maladies. However, whereas Alberdi seemed to emphasize the racial element in the Europeanizing process, (the need for a new stock of immigrants with a stress on quality rather than quantity), Sarmiento was more of a cultural Europeanizer. According to the latter, the school was conceived of as the omnipotent instrument of national reorganization. Sarmiento also looked to the United States as the model nation to be followed. Civilization was defined in terms of European institutions, and the United States was the greatest Europeanizing agent of all times. In order to "debarbarize" Argentina, Sarmiento would "North Americanize" it.

Alberdi, too, speaks of the United States in most favorable terms. "To govern is to populate" is his famous dictum, advanced in his *Bases:* to populate in the sense of improving and civilizing as is the case in the United States. Sarmiento and Alberdi, then, represent a "native" Positivism which has been designated as an "environmental and diffused"

* The Argentine dictator, Juan Manuel de Rosas, was defeated by General Justo José de Urquiza in the battle of Monte Caseros on February 3, 1852, and exiled to England.

Positivism.[42] There is also the period of "Positivism in action,"[43] a period characterized by urgent clamor for the need to educate the people, to create wealth, to harness philosophy in the service of the country's needs. According to Alberdi, philosophy is to be studied not as abstract, speculative theory, but as applied to the nation's immediate interests, i.e. "political philosophy, the philosophy of our industry and wealth, the philosophy of our literature, the philosophy of our religion and our history . . ."[44]

This "native Positivism in action," is linked with "the economic growth of the country, the predominance of material interests, the development of public education, the incorporation of heterogeneous masses, the affirmation of individual freedom."[45]

It was within this framework that Sarmiento founded the Normal School of Paraná, whose mission it was to further the education of the masses—part and parcel of Sarmiento's battle against the "barbarism" of Rosas. Popular education, political institutions, a spirit of enterprise, the predilection for technical efficiency, the accent on individual freedom—all of these were component parts of the total configuration presented by the United States, which Sarmiento admired and intended to emulate.

Can this "autochthonous" Positivism be considered a genuine part of Positivist philosophy in the strictly philosophical sense of the term? Torchia-Estrada would deny this claim. According to this contemporary Argentine philosopher, Alberdi, Sarmiento and others of this period were simply public statesmen who were imbued with a spirit of utilitarianism.[46]

One must also be careful to distinguish between Positivism, *estrictu generis*, and scientific determinism. The latter half of the 19th century and the opening decade of the 20th are characterized by a dissemination of scientific application to psychology, education, and ethics. Darwinian evolution, naturalism and biological concepts applied to morality, replace religion as determining factors in one's conception of the world and of life.

The emphasis on science—spelled with a capital "S" (which can properly be called "Scientism"), although coinciding in many cases with the advent of Positivism in Argentina, must nevertheless be kept apart from and not equated with the latter. Whereas Positivism did not provide any room within its conceptual scheme for metaphysics of any kind, "Scientism" on the other hand with its strong faith in itself, did not hesitate to speak of a metaphysics of science. This point should be kept in mind especially when we consider the first of the three principal philosophers dealt with in this study, namely, José Ingenieros.

✓ ✓ ✓

At the close of the century, then, philosophy (except in Catholic and traditionalist circles) is strongly tinged with scientific trappings. In fact, one can now speak of a scientific philosophy, i.e., a philosophy dependent upon scientific hypotheses. A metaphysics is elaborated, one based on scientific postulates. Experimentation and observation constitute the methodology whereby the "scientific" philosopher strives to achieve the absolute. The basic assumption underlying this philosophical activity is that the as yet unknown reality behaves in the same fashion as that which is already known. Florentino Ameghino is typical of this approach.

Ameghino was known chiefly for his studies in anthropology and paleontology. Strongly influenced in his thinking by Darwin and Lamarck, he arrived at conclusions similar to those of Haeckel. His early scientific writings portrayed evolutionism as an implacable opponent of theology. As a scientific materialist he placed his research activities and findings at the service of Science in its battle against Religion. "The idea of God is a primitive one, simple and infantile, a child of the fear engendered by the unknown . . ."[47]

According to Ameghino, "the existence of a creator of the Universe is incompatible with the notion of the existence of eternity of space and matter,"[48] Ameghino's *Credo,* influenced by Spencer's *First Principles,* partakes of both Positivist and evolutionary doctrines. He transforms principles derived from the material sciences into cosmological laws.

The Universe is conceived of as being composed of matter as well as space, time, and movement. All four are infinite in nature and are dependent on one another.[49]

The problems posed by Ameghino were studied assiduously by Argentine "scientism," problems which concerned themselves with the continuity between matter, life and thought, the possibility of psychological explanations based on biological facts, and the hypothesis of universal evolutionism supported by the biological sciences.

The evolutionary Positivism of Spencer subsequently pushed the Comtian variety aside. This process was aided by the diffusion of biological evolutionism at the University of Buenos Aires, where the medical and natural sciences were developed. The Argentine environment was thus permeated with a utilitarian orientation, and Argentine Positivism was channelled in the direction of a naturalist and scientific frame of reference.

✓   ✓   ✓

The Argentine "generation of 1880" was to bear witness to the so-called "alluvial era,"[50] characterized by waves of immigration. The landowning oligarchy made its appearance. So did labor unrest. In the growing gap that resulted between the mass of people and the wealthy landowners, the men of 1880 looked to Positivism as a means of not only building the country materially, but also ethically. The conduct of business and government had left much to be desired; speculation, "extravagance and corruption were unrestrained."[51]

The "generation of 1880" possessed a profound faith in the determinism of the natural sciences, as these could be applied to sociological and psychological studies. The men of this generation aspired to the utilization of empirical facts and human interaction for the purpose of formulating a political science. Experimental psychology was to reveal the necessary data with which to glimpse the spiritual life of man.

Besides the Paraná circle of Positivist thinkers men-

22

tioned above,* there were university groups at La Plata, Buenos Aires, and to a lesser extent at the University of Córdoba. The university groups seem to have preferred the agnostic and evolutionary doctrines of Spencer, i.e., to the extent to which these could be adapted to the legal, political, and educational aspects of the Argentine scene, whereas within the Paraná group Comtism prevailed. As Korn puts it: "With a horror of the metaphysical, without religious fervor, they (i.e., the university groups) accepted as dogma the subordination of the psychological to the natural sciences; they professed the individualistic tendencies of English liberalism, (and) proclaimed the excellence of the experimental method . . ."[52] Armed with the methodology of the natural sciences, the university Positivists thus proposed to study the evolution of Argentine society, to discover its laws and to solve its evils.

Pedro Scalabrini, the Italian professor who taught at Paraná, merged Darwinism with the Comtian law of the three stages, i.e., theology, metaphysics and Positivism. Scalabrini endeavored to teach according to the pattern laid down by Comte, whereby sociology and the so-called moral sciences rest on a hierarchical foundation of mathematics and natural sciences. Even so, in the educational sphere the theories of Froebel and Pestalozzi, rather than those of Comte, were advocated at the Normal School.

However, the most notable exponent of Comtian Positivism at Paraná was J. Alfredo Ferreira. For Ferreira, Positivism represents the philosophy of science, art and action. Like science, Positivism is based on the doctrine of evolution. Facts determine ideas and sentiments. The truth is arrived at by means of investigating the facts. Since the facts are themselves subject to change, nothing can be said to be stable. In ethics there are no general or abstract norms, valid for all time and in all places. "Good" and "bad" are relative concepts, determined by social conditions.[52a] The era of Absolute Truth has passed. Every day the relativity of ideas becomes clearer. The unilateral has given way to

---

* See page 20.

the multilateral. Religion, e.g., is a social product, a way of looking at the Universe. Consequently, traditional religion becomes a natural target for the Comtian Positivists at Paraná who do their utmost to stimulate and strengthen the scientific spirit. In this intellectual climate, Ferreira seeks to replace theological dogma with ethical ideals of a secular nature, thus approximating Comte's religion of humanity.

The biological foundation of ethics is one of the doctrines found in the works of Carlos Octavio Bunge. Morality is a highly relativistic concept, conditioned by the subject, his medium and the moment of action. Human behavior is motivated by the desire for self-preservation and the conservation of the species. Philogenetic evolution is very similar to the historic evolution of peoples. Both are the result of the activities of human instinct. This is the core, of Bunge's psychological theories. Instinct is the basic factor whence are derived the laws of biology, psychology and sociology. Intelligence is nothing more than an advanced stage of instinctive behavior.[53] For Bunge, nothing should be admitted which has not been proven inductively. Knowledge, not only ethics, is relative. The only absolute we accept is that everything is relative. Operating within the framework of the predominant positivist philosophy, as well as a strongly slanted bio-psychological sociology, Bunge maintained that all knowledge is derived from experience, and that our relativism makes it impossible to grasp the absolute.[54]

Some Argentine thinkers combined Spencerian Positivism with Marxist socialism. This was most curious, since the Argentine bourgeoisie had also utilized Positivist doctrines to advance its own economic interests. Whereas the bourgeoisie utilized Spencer to justify its individualism, socialist-oriented thinkers, such as Juan Justo, found in Spencer, as well as in Darwin, the necessary rationale to justify aspirations involved in the class struggle of the laboring classes.

Argentina's old struggles were now beginning to be replaced by conflicts of a new type. No longer was it a question of civilization versus barbarism, of warfare between Buenos

Aires and the provinces. That which appeared upon the horizon at this moment was class warfare. The gaucho had been vanquished by the immigrant. The industrial proletariat was now social problem Number One.

It should be pointed out, however, that Justo is considered a deviationist by orthodox Marxists. (Of course, the term "deviationist" is a highly flexible one). Perelstein, e.g., maintains that it is quite impossible to synthesize Marx and Comte. Comte had propounded the theory of the perennial and unchanging existence of two classes, the wealthy, governing class, and the one which is governed and which should consequently renounce any intention of depriving the former of its wealth and power. Such formulation is, of course, unthinkable in Marxian terms.[55]

In spite of his agreement with the general principles of Marxism, Justo, like Spencer, believes that human beings have developed and have been influenced by the same factors which have determined the evolution of all species. In Justo's thinking there is a mixture of naturalism and Darwinism. Nevertheless, he is closer to the biological than to the economic determinant of human development.

The merging of Positivism and Darwinism, as this appears in Argentina, the intermingling of socialist doctrine with Spencerian ideas, the influence of scientific naturalism, the psychological theories based on biological determinism— all of these currents can be said to have found their most eloquent representative and spokesman in José Ingenieros. He can perhaps be said to be the one thinker at the turn of the century in whom the dominant currents crystallize and find their most concentrated expression. He is the symbol *par excellence* of the era. It is to him that we now turn in an attempt to examine his teachings, the various facets of his thought which both coincide with and differ from Positivist doctrine; in short, his contribution to Argentine thought made during the first quarter of the 20th century.

CHAPTER TWO

José Ingenieros

INGENIEROS IS ONE of the most dynamic and controversial figures to appear on the Argentine scene. He is the great representative of the Spencer-Darwin synthesis and shares with Alejandro Korn the distinction of having greatly stimulated philosophical activity in his country. In Romero's opinion, he possessed a most fertile and "robust philosophic mentality."[1] Not only did philosophy claim his tireless and feverish devotion; he was no less prolific in psychology and sociology. His literary productivity resembles a vast constellation of interconnected aspects, an endless fabric of closely interwoven threads. Criminology is interrelated with social problems; ethics and morality with a philosophy of experience. His manifold activities, including his sporadic contacts with the Argentine socialist movement, his militancy often bordering on the belligerent, his penchant for the melodramatic—all of these evoked the unbounded admiration of significant segments of Latin American youth. In all probability, they also brought on his premature death.

Ingenieros' youth coincides with the twilight period of the so-called "generation of 1880,"* the group which bent all its energies, often ruthlessly so, in the direction of developing the material well-being of the country. This was the group, too, which sought to bring Argentina into line with other progressive national economies. It transformed the colonial aspect of the land and modernized the legal structure. Suspicious of the lower classes, it did its utmost

---

*See page 22.

to curtail emergent radical tendencies. In general, it represents the triumph of upper class interests, being "liberal in economics, conservative in politics."[1a]

The anti-metaphysical bias noted in the generation of 1880 was a correlative of highly utilitarian tendencies, characteristic of this period of Argentine economic development. The so-called feudal oligarchy of the interior had come to an understanding with the commercial oligarchy of Buenos Aires.[1b] Both groups encouraged the penetration of foreign capital, granting favorable concessions especially to English entrepreneurs. The evolutionary doctrines of Manchester seemed to sit well with economic expansion. The Spencerian influence crowded Comtism out of the picture. This was the immediate cultural environment in which Ingenieros found himself. He imbibed avidly at the fount of Positive "Scientism," mixed with social Darwinism. Within this milieu of economic liberalism, the budding forces of cultural liberalism were encouraged and given an opportunity to grow stronger. The natural sciences, hitherto unknown or neglected, received a healthy impetus. As has already been pointed out, Florentino Ameghino made outstanding contributions to Argentine paleontology; José María Ramos Mejía applied scientific techniques to an expanding and developing program of medical studies. Both men were to exert a significant influence upon José Ingenieros.

When Ingenieros made his appearance, the Argentine social and intellectual climate was about to be profoundly affected by two significant movements: one, literary, the other, political. Ingenieros was to participate in both. In the literary realm, the influence of the great Modernist poet, Rubén Darío, awakened Argentine youth to subtleties of tone and rhythm, suggestive nuances, symbols and imagery, as well as intellectual curiosity and disquietude.

Politically, the current which swept into the country from abroad was inspired by Marxist socialism. The cynical and gross opportunism of the "oligarchy" was offset by an idealism that appealed to sensitive youth. In this respect, Marxism can be said to have represented a continuation of an earlier brand of socialism—Saint Simonian in nature—as personified in Esteban Echeverría's *Dogma socialista.*

There was more than a fortuitous relationship between the two movements, Modernism and socialism. In many instances, the literary figures were themselves actively aligned in the ranks of those who would transform society. In both cases, established perspectives were attacked as old and outworn, and in need of replacement. Rubén Darío himself was said to have been imbued with leftist tendencies, although these were anarchist-inspired, rather than socialist.

Ingenieros had practically been born into revolutionary ideology. His father, an Italian emigré, had been editor of the first socialist newspaper in his country. The Ingenieros home in Buenos Aires soon became the gathering place of radicals of all hues. It could therefore be expected that young Ingenieros, at the age of eighteen, should be editor of a socialist-oriented university publication, *La Vanguardia,* and that two years later, he should edit the revolutionary socialist periodical, *La Montaña.*[1c]

A group of young *literati,* labelled *La Syringa* by Darío,[1d] delighted in poking fun mercilessly at all the human foibles on the Argentine scene. Its favorite weapon was devastating irony, its outstanding characteristic supreme self-confidence, its undisputed leader José Ingenieros. Perhaps this was the result of the heady wine which the young men had imbibed upon discovering Nietzsche's Superman. Ingenieros' generation appeared captivated by the sense of exultation, found in the pages of *Zarathustra*: the overbubbling energy of unbridled optimism, the triumph of individual will, the resistance to the State, and the rebellion against all dogma and hypocrisy. All of these qualities, in varying degree, were to be everpresent in Ingenieros' works.

In spite of the fact that Ingenieros is placed historically within the general framework of Argentine Positivism, he is more the scientist than the Positivist. For Positivism, with its decided aversion for metaphysics, and rejecting as it does, all *a priori* concepts, stresses relativistic historicity; our knowledge of phenomena is relative to our situation. Our ideas, both individual and social, are contingent upon the conditions of our existence.

Ingenieros, too, opposed all philosophy which tends to stress the supernatural, the transcendental. Yet he was not opposed to metaphysics; in fact it takes a metaphysics to reject one. He not only recognized the possibility, but also the need for a metaphysics. But not a metaphysics based on *a priori* thinking. Ingenieros' metaphysics was to depend exclusively on experience, or rather, putting it negatively, on what we have not yet experienced. In short, the inexperienced is a constant factor, a perennial margin of our existence. This is the realm on which a metaphysics can be founded, but one which will make use of logical hypotheses, objective, scientific and anti-dogmatic formulations.

Ingenieros was a voracious reader and a prolific writer. It should not surprise us, therefore, to find in his work traces of European thought representing several countries: e.g., Bacon, Locke, and Spencer; Comte and Taine; Ostwald, Haeckel and Mach. His *Principles of Psychology,* he claims, is but an introduction to the study of psychology. He examines in this work the genesis and formation of psychic foundations in the evolution of living beings, of human societies, of individuals. Utilizing the genetic approach, Ingenieros considers psychology to be a natural science, resting on the premises of the biological sciences. He takes up in succession the natural formation of living matter, the conscious personality and the function of thinking. The theory of knowledge, the function of thought, the formation of human consciousness—all of these have evolved genetically, and can be explained satisfactorily only in terms of a naturalist philosophy.

The genetic approach to psychology views as absurd the notion that man possesses a faculty known as intelligence which specializes in knowledge and is superior to and independent of his other faculties. The genetic approach considers "faculty psychology" to be merely a tool in the hands of idealistic philosophers to further their "spiritualist beliefs." These will be replaced in the future with "functional hypotheses" which will not contradict experience.[2]

Since the function of thought is an elaboration of experiential data, it follows that, like experience upon which it is based, it will be fluid and in a state of continual change. There is no such thing as "pure thought" in and of itself, abstract and impersonal, as the old rationalist metaphysics would have us believe. Thought is concrete, performed by human beings who engage in this process in order to survive. ". . . To think means to better the conditions of adaptation and struggle for life by the species or the individuals."[3]

This genetic point of view is thus opposed to rationalist philosophy, which had always presented "reason" as a mysterious faculty whose purpose it was to think the truth and to distinguish man from other animal species.

Within the basic framework of naturalism, it is to be expected that Ingenieros should consider human consciousness as a function determined by the natural and continuous development of the individual. It is not a substance, existing as a separate entity; it is rather consciousness of "something." The influence of Ostwald's "energetist" doctrines is quite pronounced in Ingenieros' psychology. In the process of interaction between the organism and its environment there take place changes in the energy equilibrium of both. This biological operation is the basis for all psychic functions.

The doctrine of monist evolution, as interpreted genetically and to which Ingenieros subscribes, postulates the unity and continuity of matter in its various forms, especially in its vital and psychic manifestations. Moreover, bio-chemical data establish the structural as well as the functional continuity of matter. This would imply the functional continuity leading from the inorganic to the organic. The formation of organic matter is explained by the organization of atomic-molecular structures and by the acquisition of functional properties in the course of the evolutionary process.[4]

Matter and life are expressions of energy. The atomic-molecular structure of matter becomes more complex as

objects ascend the evolutionary ladder. There is uninter-
rupted continuity of structure and function, which implies
transformation of energy, i.e., change in atomic-molecular
structure. Between the specific varieties of the inorganic
and those of the organic there is no clear, neat line of demarcation. In other words, matter is one. The transition in the
evolutionary continuity is so subtle that the transition from
the inert to the vital as well as from organic to psychic
phenomena is infinitesimal. Life was born from dead matter.
It is only structure that distinguishes the two.

Energy, then, is the universal reality. Energy reactions
include not only the physical and biological but also the
psychic. But this energy, this all-inclusive concept which sets
out to explain everything—material as well as spiritual data
—what is it? Actually, Ingenieros does not define energy for
us. This is one of the complaints registered by a compatriot
of his who has studied him quite closely.[5] The notion of
energy seems to be a convenient response to our need for
explaining phenomena in terms of cause and effect.

The action of the environment upon the organism, i.e.,
"excitation," provokes the latter's reaction, or "movement."
This relationship is the origin of psychic functions which develop via the evolution of the species, the social evolution
of human beings, and the individual evolution of man. Any
excitation related to previous experience results in sensation.[6]
However, according to Torchia Estrada, Ingenieros fails to
explain satisfactorily how psychic phenomena, besides being
media for adaptation, are also perceived consciously, or, in
other words, "how *excitation* is transformed into sensation."[7]

The reaction of the organism to its environment is one
of adaptation. Both psychic and biological functions from
which the former are derived are means of adaptation. In
other words, the general conditions found within the biological frame of reference determine the appearance of psychic
functions in living matter. These functions are but responses
to environmental stimuli, or in short, means of adaptation
on the part of the living organism. Among these functions,

memory is the most important. Ingenieros resorts to memory as a means of explaining consciousness. "Excitation," or action of the environment upon the organism, is related to other stimuli and is therefore made conscious in terms of its relation to past experience. This past experience is systematized by memory. Memory is a factor which has evolved out of experience which, in turn, is a natural product of the evolutionary process. The chief function of experience and memory is to protect individuals, groups and species. Memory, then, is the faculty of preserving a structural change effected as a result of a previous energy imbalance, and experience is the sum of these changes in equilibrium, preserved by memory.

Memory also makes possible the formation of habits; the latter are means of adaptation. The constancy of the conditions which encourage the acquisition of these habits leads to their repetition and to their adoption by other individuals. The structural and functional variations which result are transmitted to future generations. Groups of tendencies or predispositions created by habit in individuals are usually called instincts when applied to a given species. Or, in other words, instincts are habits which are repeated successfully in the evolution of the species. Habits, in turn, are the results of converting into automatic, i.e., unthinking behavior, experiences which were originally intelligent, i.e., thinking and conscious behavior. Instinct, then, is experience "made automatic" by repetition within the species, whereas intelligence is aptitude for new experience.

In considering the factor of consciousness, Ingenieros seems to find himself involved in a contradiction. The possibility of a maximum of consciousness, he maintains, corresponds to a maximum of experience. The extent of consciousness possible in each individual depends on his impressions systematized previously into habits, as well as hereditary tendencies acquired by his species.[8] However, a question may be raised at this point: does consciousness depend on habit formation or is it, rather, the other way around? It would seem from the above, that habit conditions or determines consciousness, yet it is also equivalent to automatic or unconscious behavior, the result of converting thinking into unthinking behavior. The greater the span of experience and the corresponding extent of consciousness, the larger the number of habits. Thus Dujovne asks with some justification: "Is conscious behavior, i.e., purposive and thinking behavior, the product of habit or is habit equal to unconscious automatism?"[9] In short, do habits differ on the conscious or unconscious level?

Ingenieros does not seem to be bothered by this difficulty. "Consciousness" as such does not exist. If it does, it is only an objectified abstraction. It exists only as a common quality of certain psychic phenomena called the conscious. What is generally considered "consciousness" is for Ingenieros a "conscious personality," an individual ego.[10] The conscious personality develops in individuals in proportion to the degree of experience of the respective species. Intelligence and thought are linked to consciousness. Intelligence is not the opposite of instinct. It is incorrect to limit instinct to animals and intelligence to man, for both exist in man and animal, and both evolve.

Thought also, like consciousness and intelligence, does not exist in abstract form as a separate entity divorced from life, but is a result of the evolution of the species and of the struggle to adapt. It is the result of experience in that it elaborates experimental data and is equally variable. The process of thinking is part of the entire configuration of psychic factors which are themselves component parts of a unitary biological process. The various modes of thinking evolve in the course of development of the species. These forms vary in each society and attain a different level of development in each individual.[11]

One of the by-products of thought is the formation of beliefs and judgments, which are themselves subject to modification, just as is the case with reality upon which these judgments are based. Beliefs do not necessarily represent exact knowledge of reality, but rather a judgment thereof, subject to revision in the light of subsequent experience.[12]

✓ ✓ ✓

Three steps can be discerned in the philosophical writings of Ingenieros. In the first, the scientific orientation constitutes the point of departure for his venture into philosophy. His *Principles of Psychology,* as well as his commentaries on Le Dantec and Ribot, are typical of this period. The second stage of which his *Propositions Relative to the Future of Philosophy* is the culminating point, represents the basis of a "metaphysics of experience." The third period is characterized by polemical essays and critical articles concerning Kant, Croce, Gentile, and especially Boutroux.

The road to philosophy, for Ingenieros, leads from psychology through the labyrinth of sociology, both conditioned by a strongly naturalist, biological orientation. In his *Principles of Psychology,* we perceive the beginnings of what was to develop later into his full-blown, mature philosophical ideas. Psychology is "a natural science in conformity with the more general hypotheses of the biological sciences."[13] In what seems more like a philosophy of psychology, Ingenieros utilizes the biological approach to prove that human experience and the struggle for existence condition not only group and individual psychology, but also customs and ethics. Knowledge of reality is a natural result of experience: it is not the function of a "faculty of cognition" removed from reality itself.[14] It is therefore relative and limited, attaining its most complex form in the human species. Since all experiential data are empirical, it is absurd to speak of *a priori* factors and conditions, extrinsic to the experiential field itself.

Yet in the course of biological evolution, some human beings, more so than others, are capable of reliving impressions of a past reality. "Remembrance of things past," by means of a creative imagination, combines with present-day reality and is capable of projecting a vision of the future. This activity, itself a result of experience, makes it possible for more gifted individuals to transcend their present experiential state, while concomitantly basing themselves thereon, in order to anticipate future experiential data. Here we have in embryonic form the basis of an

34

ethics which Ingenieros was to develop in his subsequent writings.

One must insure, however, that human imagination never lose contact with knowledge of reality or, in short, with experience. Any problem that fails to be couched in terms of either actual or possible experience, escapes scientific treatment. The function of philosophy has always been to deal with problems of the universe. Nowadays, knowledge of the universe is more intimately related to the realm of the experiential, a realm in which the sciences play an ever increasing role. As a result, we are faced with "the possibility of a scientific philosophy," or what may be called a "true metaphysics of experience."[15] This, of course, can never be a fixed and rigid system; it is rather in continuous flux and never-ceasing formation, as mobile as the very experiences and generalizations which constitute its bases.

Ingenieros is not only polemical. At times he is somewhat aggressive and acid-tongued, a characteristic of radical and extremely self-assured innovators who arrive upon the historical scene with a new broom, ready to clean up with missionary zeal. In his opening chapter, e.g., of his *Propositions,* he speaks of the "hypocrisy of the philosophers."[16] In the past, philosophy, especially metaphysics, has been characterized by obscure terminology, by an attempt to conform to the prevailing ideas and beliefs of the times. Philosophical doctrines are incomprehensible if they are divorced from the political and religious history of the society in which they are produced.[17] Since the Renaissance, philosophers have been hypocritical because they preferred peace and success, and because they sought to avoid the persecution which their ideas might bring them. The principle of authority sealed their heretical mouths and prevented them from uttering "dangerous truths." The field was thus left open for the propagation of popular beliefs and superstitions.[18]

If, at the time of the Renaissance, the theory of double verity permitted philosophic heresy and theological dogmatism to exist side by side, in more recent times freedom

35

to investigate the truth is permitted on the one hand, while on the other, the socio-ethical consequences of these investigations are denied.[19]

Ingenieros leaves the reader with the distinct impression that this philosophical "hypocrisy" was a deliberate affair. Certainly he must have known that science was not yet sufficiently strong, its prestige still too weak and inadequate, to combat successfully the dogmatic nature of the dominant intellectual structure of that period. Many of the principles which we now take for granted had not yet appeared, or else, were still in embryonic form. Ingenieros would have done well to substitute "ignorance" for "hypocrisy."

Ingenieros utilizes "experience" as the primary factor in erecting his philosophical structure. Ethics, logic and esthetics are reduced to the psychological which rests on biological foundations. Metaphysics is the only branch of philosophy which cannot be reduced to science and therefore becomes synonymous with philosophy itself.

The crisis in 19th century philosophy was due to a clash of two disciplines. On the one hand, idealistic philosophers refused to incorporate the results of experience into their metaphysical framework. On the other hand, men of science riding the crest of the onrushing "scientific" tide, repudiated any idea not empirically demonstrable. Ingenieros himself scoffed at those who believed that science could resolve all enigmas.

The divorce between science and philosophy caused the metaphysicians to reserve unto themselves the terrain of the absolute, since it was obvious that science was operating exclusively in the field of the relative, of the experiential.

Metaphysics, then, suffered a double blow: Positivism had cast it aside; so had spiritualism which became transformed into mysticism.[20] Ingenieros found himself at the crossroads. "The generation prior to mine has passed through two stages: the positivist and the mystical. My generation has experienced more particularly the second stage. I never attained the first, nor have I succumbed to the second."[21]

Metaphysics embraces the inexperiential. No matter how much progress is made by science, there will always be an inexhaustible residue left, dealing with what has not yet been experienced. "Inexperiential" does not refer to the nature of objects but rather to our knowledge. It has nothing in common with the "supernatural," with the pantheistic absolute, with the *a priori* "transcendental," with the "unintelligible" of the relativists, nor finally with the "unknowable" of the agnostics.[22] All of these are noumenal, as opposed to the phenomenal which is rooted in experience.

Objects are variable in time and space. So is our experience. Once the problem is stated in these terms, it becomes evident that the experiential is infinitely variable. It is likewise evident that any metaphysics, i.e., any hypotheses postulated in scientific terms which rest on what is already known, if applied to what is not yet known, will likewise be subject to modification and control. This, then, is a philosophy based on science, conceived in terms of legitimate hypotheses which rest on the results of experience, a philosophy which undertakes to interpret problems which lie outside the experiential realm.

Sciences are systems of truths which are constantly less imperfect. The idea of absolute principles is an absurdity. In this way, Ingenieros seeks to bridge the gap between science and philosophy. The agent which will effect this sought-after arrangement is human imagination. Creative imagination, based on experience, is the origin of all hypotheses; it seeks to transcend the area of the known and explore that of the unknown, the realm of metaphysics. Experience has shown that philosophy has not always maintained this necessary connecting link with science. The result has been the formulation of illegitimate hypotheses.

Science and philosophy, then, are not mutually antagonistic. In fact, philosophy cannot isolate itself from science. The universe consists of relationships which are incessantly variable. The possibility of total knowledge of these variables becomes strong only if we believe that the universe will stop evolving and reach a state of inertia in the face of continuous advance by human experience. Since this prospect has very slim possibilities, the implication is obvious: our experience is much less than the variability of objects and relationships. We will, therefore, always be confronted by a residue of the inexperiential.[23] "The infinite possibility of problems which exceed human experience implies the perennial state of hypothetical explanations which constitute a metaphysics."[24]

In the metaphysics of the future, proclaims Ingenieros confidently, "false problems" will be eliminated with increasing frequency.[25] This will be a welcome change from what was characteristic, e.g., of medieval metaphysics which was subordinated to theology.

Beginning with the Renaissance, philosophy made efforts to regain its autonomy. Unfortunately, its leading exponents were not brave enough to free themselves from popular superstitions. All forms of rationalism, e.g., have been transitional forms, i.e., between the philosophy of the past and that of the future, between what was no longer worthy of credence and that to which no one was as yet bold enough to give utterance.[26]

✓ ✓ ✓

The three classic problems, namely, God, immortality and freedom, are excluded from the domain of Ingenieros' metaphysics. These are simply leftovers from medieval scholasticism, since "they do not attempt to explain that which arises out of experience, but rather to confirm a given system of popular beliefs."[27]

Pantheists comprise one of several groups which come in for a tongue lashing. Their position is "hypocritical" because in applying the name of God to nature, they are guilty of retaining a word which is commonly applied to a hypothetical being distinct from Nature. There is evident here a certain degree of "immorality," since the philosophers in question are guilty of perpetuating deceit. Humanity has for countless centuries—due to the heritage of mysticism—entertained a profound aversion for atheism. Many idealistic philosophers, as well as Positivists, have been guilty of insincerity due to the fact that they have used obscure language in order to disguise their true opinions.[28]

In the same belligerent tone, Ingenieros asserts that no longer does anyone speak of "soul" and "immortality." Instead, it is more sophisticated to refer to "spirit." This adds to the general confusion, since "soul" and "reason" are confounded. The problem concerning immortality of the soul is not legitimate as a metaphysical hypothesis since it is a mystical rather than a rational belief.[29]

Similarly, "free will" has been replaced by "contingency" and "indeterminism." To say that only the First Cause is free and that men have subsequently been determined thereby, amounts to word play. Another example: man was born free, but was subsequently enslaved by his appetites; or, some men were born with "grace," but not others. This is the height of absurdity.[30]

The three problems, then, associated with classical metaphysics, namely, God, immortality of the soul and freedom, derive from *a priori* conceptions. They constitute a residue of medieval scholasticism, and have no authoritative basis from the scientific point of view. They cannot be demonstrated by experience or the experimental method and are therefore "illegitimate" problems. Yet as he examines them, Ingenieros concludes that they are not completely devoid of legitimate content. It is just that their "illegitimate" character derives from the fact that they have been formulated incorrectly. Since they have evolved and undergone modification, there is still an element of "legitimacy" within each of them.

Some of the problems which are subsumed under these three categories and which Ingenieros designates as "legitimate" involve the nature of substance, nature in all of its known, experiential aspects, the origin and purpose of life, the possibility of life on other planets, and the relationship between mental processes and organic activity. And he concludes confidently: "I believe that in the future the results grounded in experience will define the limits and legitimate conditions of those problems which are inexperiential."[31]

And how is this to be done? Simply by appealing to the principle of "that which cannot be."[32] In other words, experience cannot determine the truth of what is not experienced. But it can eliminate illegitimate problems. This points essentially to the difference between scientific and metaphysical hypotheses. The former can be proved experientially; the latter are only judgments of probability. As one critic has pointed out, the exactitude of metaphysical postulates cannot be shown by having recourse to experience; however, "their legitimacy is logically demonstrable."[33] The perfectibility of human experience never quite excludes the perennial quality of an as yet inexperienced residue."[34]

The implication is clear: this residue of the non-experienced insures a permanent metaphysics. As long as problems exist which surpass human experience, so long as the variability of objects and their circumstances is greater than the possibility of that experience, just so long will there be hypothetical explanations and attempts at interpretations. These, in the last analysis, constitute a metaphysics.[35]

For man, the difference between reality and its appearance will continue to be an "inexperiential" problem. But any subsequent hypothesis, in order to be legitimate, must be in accord with all prior experiential data; it becomes illegitimate when it resorts to *a priori*, abstract and "pure" ideas.[36] All inexperiential hypotheses will evolve continually within the context of experiential media.

Metaphysics, then, seems to become an extension of science. Metaphysical hypotheses begin where science, availing itself of experiential hypotheses, can no longer operate. Metaphysics prolongs itself "legitimately" in the terrain of the inexperiential.[37]

The "legitimate" methods to be used in the formulation of a "metaphysics of the future" involve methodical doubt of the results of observation and experiment since these are also conditioned on the assumption that they are incomplete.

Moreover, this type of metaphysics requires the formulation of hypotheses which explain experimental results and the willingness to question these hypotheses in order to determine their legitimacy in accordance with the results of experience. "This methodological process establishes a natural continuity between the scientific and the metaphysical hypotheses."[38] The methodology of the new metaphysics will, of course, exclude intuitive and mystical approaches, since these are not subject to experimental control.

The metaphysics which Ingenieros advocates will possess the same characteristics as are to be found in science: universality, perfectibility, (i.e., a continually evolving open system), antidogmatism, and, finally, an increasing degree of impersonality in the sense that a greater number of competent individuals will participate in its elaboration.[39] There will no longer be any distinction between the natural sciences and the "cultural" or "normative" sciences. Nor will there be a dual system of verities. No contradictory truths, no dangerous truths, no truths to be sacrificed.

When Ingenieros tells us that there will always be inexperiential problems rooted in the experiential, whose *raison d'être* becomes the object of his metaphysical study, he would naturally be expected to elucidate as to the nature of these problems. Yet one looks in vain for further elaboration and clarification. What are these problems? What do they consist of? True, he states that these relate to the perfectibility of human experience, to the further enrichment of knowledge. Yet is this radically new? Hasn't metaphysics always aimed in this direction, to attempt to explain what lies beyond the world of the senses? At least one contemporary philosopher issues a similar complaint: there is nothing terribly original in this. Even idealist philosophy, the target of Ingenieros' polemics has, since Kant, admitted an infinite realm that cannot be grasped in its totality, yet which has constantly served to stimulate human effort, resulting in scientific progress.[40]

Ingenieros, therefore, in spite of himself, seems to be closer to the idealists whom he attacks, than he perhaps

41

realizes or cares to admit. For doesn't he affirm the infinite possibility of problems which lie outside the realm of human experience and which therefore imply the perennial nature of hypothetical explanations? Does the perennially known and stable always condition the unstable and unknown? Is there not the possibility that the reverse may also operate at times, namely, that the unstable and the unknown may conceivably condition the stable and the known?

Moreover, when he tells us that the experiential will provide us with hypotheses with which to project ourselves into the realm of the inexperiential—and that only these hypotheses will be legitimate precisely because they are based on experience—does he define "legitimacy?" In other words, he excludes "illegitimate" premises without telling us anything about the "legitimate" ones, although he says that "experience can limit and condition non-experience by the principle of non-contradiction, which shows *that which cannot be.*"[41]

It would be absurd for experience to judge the truth of that which refers to the non-experienced. But what is experienced can allow for the establishment of the *illegitimate* nature of certain problems, and thus exclude them from metaphysics. In short, "it authorizes the elimination of illegitimate problems although it may not decide on the truth of legitimate hypotheses."[42]

Can it be that as he enmeshed himself in this labyrinth of contradictions—and perhaps he himself realized it—that he was, as Alejandro Korn suggests, desperately looking for something which he was at the same time rejecting, because of his anti-theological bias?

✓   ✓   ✓

Philosophy is a method of criticism. Moreover, it is to be distinguished from science in that it "tends to be a generalization of generalizations . . . a criticism of criticisms, an hypothesis of hypotheses."[43] Because it is a scientific philosophy it can, thanks to the findings of psychology and biology, formulate hypotheses concerning such problems as

42

the formation of matter, of personality, and even the nature and function of thinking.

Scientific philosophy is conceived of as an organization of legitimate assumptions which are in harmony with the general results of experience; it is, furthermore, a system which would endeavor to explore and interpret problems which are as yet outside the realm of experience, a system in continuous formation. "It has methods, but no dogmas. It is self-correcting to the extent that the rhythm of experience varies ... it represents an unstable equilibrium between experience which grows and hypotheses which are corrected."[44]

Whatever the hypotheses and generalizations that may be formed, these will always be provisional and transitory. Men of science, in Ingenieros' time, seemed so obsessed with the specific, enmeshed as they were in their narrow generalizations; they refused to consider or deal with the philosophical implications of their work. Ingenieros therefore pointed to the necessity for Argentine Positivists to free themselves from an excessive preoccupation with the concrete, a preoccupation which had been cultivated in the name of science.[45] Some would even accept the findings of science, but would then utilize these as premises or points of departure from which to apply their intuitive method. As for intuition, it is quite impossible to define this concept in a manner so as to satisfy all people, since the adherents of intuitionism cannot agree among themselves as to the findings of their intuition. Intuition has its values in the esthetic realm, in the world of artistic imagination, but not as a tool with which to investigate the truth.

Speculative and intuitive philosophy has always assigned different methods to science and philosophy, respectively. With the passage of time, however, Ingenieros feels that one method alone will suffice to know reality, a method which will go beyond narrow empiricism, allowing for imaginative hypotheses, while, at the same time, opposed to intuitionism because it denies that intuition can arrive at truths without the benefit of suppositions which concur with the

43

results of experience. This new method will likewise be opposed to rationalism which claims to operate according to laws that lie outside the realm of experience.

The growth and development of both natural sciences and philosophy are realized as a function of the medium within which they take place, i.e., they are determined by social experience. For this reason, Ingenieros criticizes Kant in rather harsh terms. Instead of interpreting knowledge as a natural result of experience, Kant converted the function of knowing into an entity removed from and superior to experience. Kant's *Critique of Practical Reason,* asserts Ingenieros, is a naive attempt to reconcile reason and superstition and to reach an agreement between the logical and the absurd. It is a "monumental homage to popular beliefs."[46]

Anticipating what was to appear several years later in more elaborate fashion (*Propositions ...*), Ingenieros sustains the need for the formation and perpetuation of ideals. His ideal-ism (as opposed to idea-lism) is of course founded on experience in keeping with his general schemata.

An ideal is also an hypothesis, the loftiest result of the function of thought. Human imagination, basing itself upon experience, elaborates beliefs concerning future perfection. Human evolution is characterized by a continual effort on the part of man to adapt himself to nature which, in turn, also develops and undergoes changes. In the process, man needs to know his surrounding reality and to envisage his future, ever-improving adaptations. The successive stages, as conceived by the human mind, are known as "ideals." "An ideal is a point and a moment among the possible infinites which inhabit time and space."[47] In his *Propositions* he tells us that an ideal is "a hypothetical archetype of perfection, abstracted from experience."[48] In its formulation a dual process is involved: the elimination of particular imperfections, and the synthesis of all conceivable perfections, i.e., those which are an outgrowth of experience. These hypothetical archetypes can therefore be considered legitimate beliefs; they are illegitimate if they run counter to experience.

44

However, these ideals and beliefs are not universal. "Each individual, group, class, nation, race, undergoes a different experience and evolves thereby an hypothesis of perfection which is necessarily different."[49]

In accordance with Ingenieros' evolutionary approach, the most legitimate ideals will survive in the process of natural selection. Even though beliefs and ideals will be colored by ethics and national considerations, "everything leads one to believe that in civilized humanity ideals tend toward a progressive universality."[50] These will be ideals, common to enlightened citizens of all nations without regard to geographical boundaries.

Ideals, then, are never *a priori*. They are akin to a state of equilibrium that exists between the past and the future. They are abstracted from daily deeds and facts, and constitute assumptions concerning ceaseless change. They are beliefs which influence our behavior to the degree that we believe in them. "The future is identified with the perfect. And ideals, by being visions which anticipate that which is yet to be, influence behavior and are the natural instrument of all human progress."[51]

In short, ideals evolve as a function of adaptation to future variations. They are the products of men who can visualize, foresee, think and imagine, instrumentalities utilized as mechanisms for adapting oneself to the environment. These projected hypotheses or archetypes of behavior are not inflexible; they are relative. Human beings have to adapt themselves to situations which are themselves undergoing continual change.

This experiential idealism is opposed to the dogmatic idealism of the old metaphysicians, inherent in the absolute and *a priori* "ideas." To reduce idealism to dogma is to emasculate it. And yet one perceives a contradiction in the philosophical position assumed by Ingenieros. For in his *Psychology* he opposes man's free will. "Customs," he writes, "as revealed by reality are mental habits acquired collectively by each society, and play a protective role . . .

for the preservation of the group . . ."[52] Morality, then, is but a biological function.

It would seem that at this point the two facets of Ingenieros' personality come into conflict with each other: his deterministic bias in philosophy versus his generous striving toward the good; his "science" versus his ethics. Well might one ask, together with Torchia-Estrada: "How is one to explain the drive toward moral perfection, if man is ruled by a rigorous determinism and lacks the freedom to choose the road toward perfecting himself?"[53]

Is not one brought face to face, then, with this basic inconsistency? On the one hand, eloquent addresses directed to the youth of Latin America, calculated to awaken and inspire them with lofty, idealistic sentiments; on the other, the assertion that ethics are simply a means of insuring biological survival.

✓ ✓ ✓

Ingenieros admired particularly the French philosopher, Le Dantec, for whom the solution to all problems is governed by a rigid determinism. He found in Le Dantec that spirit of combativeness to which he was so attached, a spirit that waged war on intuitive and mystical philosophies which in his opinion, placed sentimentalities above truth. In his lecture on Le Dantec (1917), held at a time when the philosophy of Bergson seemed to be gaining ground, Ingenieros boldly attacked what he considered to be the force of obscurantism in philosophy.

In the aforementioned lecture, delivered on the occasion of the death of Le Dantec, Ingenieros returns again to the basic theme: experience determines our mode of thinking, our morality. Unfortunately the vast majority of mankind is still incapable of realizing that morality is a product of social interaction, that it is grounded in social rather than supernatural sanctions. This common error accounts for the lack of progress in philosophy. "The unawareness of this evident fact (i.e., that social sanctions are more efficient) and the persistent interest in ignoring it, destroy the progress of contemporary science and philosophy."[54]

46

Science as well as philosophy will always consist of a system of modifiable hypotheses subject to continuous improvement. In the eyes of Ingenieros, Le Dantec is a champion who represents biological determinism, sallying forth boldly to storm the ramparts of vitalism. The works of the Frenchman served to spur him on to greater efforts to demolish what he considered an untenable double standard, namely, determinism in science and indeterminism in matters of the spirit. Le Dantec himself had labeled this attitude as hypocritical. One cannot have it both ways. One either is or isn't determinist all the way down the line, consistently, in every area.[55]

Even though Ingenieros left the Socialist Party in 1899, almost two decades later in his Le Dantec lecture he speaks of religion as being "a first-rate instrument in the service of the conservative class of society."[56] When Darwinism threatened the foundation of religion, the Church undertook a counter-attack: to prove that there were men of science who did not believe in evolution, that there was another more "prudent" kind of science, one which defended the dogmas threatened by the "heretical" variety.[57]

In his essay on Le Dantec, Ingenieros refers again to his theory of knowledge. Either we believe that all knowledge is a result of experience of the individual as well as of the species, or we postulate the possibility that there are ways and means of knowing which are removed from or exist prior to experience. These two alternatives are essentially what distinguishes the materialist from the supernaturalist.[58]

If we assert that natural laws known by man are a product of his experience, then it follows that all problems are transposed from the realm of the mystical and the supernatural to the natural, realistic frame of reference.

In view of the above, Ingenieros' position on atheism should not surprise anyone. People have an inordinate horror of atheism. For centuries on end, they have believed in the existence of supernatural beings who play a role in their progress or lack thereof. Human beings hope and pray for

47

rewards bestowed upon them by these gods and fear punishment at their hands. "All forms of Theism, from the most sublime to the most ridiculous . . . constitute the *world of the supernatural* in which the religious experience of humanity evolves."[59] Real, convinced atheists are rare. The attitude of awe and wonderment in the face of the unknown has engendered the formation of mystical feelings. These have acted as deterrents to logical thinking.

Ingenieros adduces the rather curious argument that pantheistic philosophers are the only true, rational atheists, but that they have always preferred to hide and disguise their opinions. Pantheism is a clever technique utilized for the purpose of not having to believe in supernatural gods; its adherents pretend, instead, to believe in one God which encompasses within itself all of nature. Le Dantec did not incur in this bit of hypocrisy. He dealt with the problem of divinity in the same way and with the same methods that he used in, let us say, studying a mushroom!

There are no proofs for the existence of God. They are as unnecessary for those who believe in Him, as for those who do not believe. This is all a matter of temperament and education. The idea of God in the mind of an educated theologian is quite different from that of a bigot in a backward village. The former would probably blush with shame and squirm uncomfortably at the conception held by the latter; the latter would probably reciprocate by viewing the former as a dangerous heretic.

The problem is pragmatic rather than one which involves logic. It is a question of the social implications of atheism. The upper classes have always preferred to foment the religiosity of the people, promising them happiness in the next world. In this way, their desire for happiness in this world is dulled and weakened; it becomes easier to manage them. Furthermore, it is absurd to think that it is possible to convert individuals of a mystical temperament to atheism by using a rational approach. "These are born believers and they can only change gods . . ."[60]

Morality is a product of social experience. It can be

defined as a system of concessions, offered in reciprocal fashion, which men have derived from group living in order to insure the best possibilities for individual existence. In biological terms, it can be said that individual morality consists in reducing to a minimum one's own evil tendencies with respect to one's fellow man, and that social morality is nothing more than the lessening of prejudices found in the social unit, which can harm the individuals who comprise it. This, in a nutshell, is the meaning of virtue and justice![61]

There is a moral premise underlying the method of investigating truth: not to submit to group superstitions, and not to fear the consequences of knowing the truth. Any branch of knowledge which is hamstrung by factors alien thereunto, is not *bona fide* knowledge; it is an enemy of truth. The true scholar and man of science does not say what others would like to hear, but rather what he himself believes. "There are no conventional truths; the only thing which is conventional is falsehood, hypocrisy."[62]

Although his affiliation with the Socialist Party of Argentina was brief (being limited to his early years), Ingenieros continued for years afterward to show evidence of socialist influence. Not only had he read Marx and Engels; he had also studied critics and commentators of Marxist thought. Using the Comtian formula, he asserted that socialism had undergone three stages of development: 1. the utopian phase, i.e., equivalent to the theoretical stage; 2. the empirical or so-called "scientific" stage, as elaborated by Marx and Engels; and 3. the "critical" and "practical" period which is really the scientific and highest phase.

According to Agosti, who criticizes him for exhibiting "revisionist tendencies,"[63] it appears that Ingenieros would merge socialist doctrine with positivist thinking. For the Marxist phase, corresponding essentially to the "metaphysical" stage, prepared the terrain so that socialism could lead into determinism. The third and last period, characterized by criticism of Marx, made it possible for socialist doctrine to adapt itself "to the necessities of positivist politics."[64]

Ingenieros' conception of historical evolution gradually became divested of the orthodox rigidity, characteristic of his youthful proclamations. In accordance with the genetic approach, he maintained that economic factors were merely a particular instance of more-inclusive biological laws, an example, applied to the human species, of principles which dictate the struggle for existence in the animal kingdom. According to this formulation, sociology would be akin to a natural science which studies the evolution of the human species under conditions which are propitious to its continued existence. Needs common to all living matter determine the struggle for life. In human beings, these needs are modified and conditioned by associations and relationships: races of mankind, social groups which comprise the race, classes within each group, and finally, individuals who are part of the group.

Any modification in the organization of the social unit is a result of changes which take place in the environment—spatially and temporally. This, in turn, determines corresponding variations in the mentality of the group, which appear in the form of attitudes, beliefs and customs.

Applied specifically to the Argentine scene, and brought out in Ingenieros' *Sociología argentina,* this perspective points to development in two directions: 1. in the internal sense, the evolution of indigenous barbarism toward a civilization cast in European terms, and 2. the development, from an international point of view, from a state of colonial feudalism to one of democratic orientation which should act as an example for other South American countries.

Vitally interested in the problems of his country, Ingenieros never missed an opportunity to instruct, elevate and inspire. For example, upon his triumphal return from Rome in 1906, where he had participated as the official Argentine delegate to an international conference on psychology, Ingenieros struck a nostalgic, yet colorful, note:

> To love one's homeland is to bestow dignity upon oneself. To fortify the trunk of the tree which affords its

shade to all of us is a means of experiencing the highest type of patriotism. Let us all try to be vigorous cells of this growing organism . . . Let us be like tiles, each of which in its distinct way combines to form the mosaic of nationality; let us all be diverse in size, shape, color and brilliance, but all of us harmoniously constituted within the grandiose end result of the whole . . . Let us aspire to create a national science, a national art, a national feeling, adapting the characteristics of the original, multiple races to the framework of our physical and social environment. Just as every man aspires to stand out in his family group, every family in its class, every class within its people, so, similarly, let our people be someone worthwhile within humanity.[64a]

This interest in the tone, color and essence of his country, in the national *ethos,* was further revealed in the commentary offered by Ingenieros concerning the psychological configuration of the Argentine gaucho. In 1906, upon the centenary of Argentine independence, a wave of unhealthy nostalgia for the gaucho as a national archetype swept the country. Juan Moreira, the legendary gaucho and representative of rural nativism, was invested with all the attributes of a national hero;[64b] this, in spite of the fact that Juan Moreira, popularized in the early Argentine theater, was the personification of rebellion against authority.

Ingenieros undertook to explode the myth. The cult of male virility and courage, the image of the noble bandit "à la Robin Hood"—all this was completely erroneous. The numerous assassinations perpetrated by Juan Moreira were not deeds of heroism, but on the contrary, acts of cowardice, motivated solely by the desire to rob and plunder. Juan Moreira had never known any friends; he had only accomplices. Far from being a rebel, he was a servile instrument, used by local politicians who were dishonest and unscrupulous, especially at election time. Nor was he a romantic balladeer; his specialty was gambling. In short, Juan Moreira was an unfortunate product of adverse conditions, inherent in the barbaric pampas.

This idealization, Ingenieros continued, could be most unfortunate for Argentina. What the country needed was to be educated to appreciate courage and valor, but in more civilized forms. "There is greater bravery in the teacher who imparts knowledge, in the worker who produces, in the scholar who studies, and in the woman who knows how to be a mother, than in the wild beast, adept only at gorging itself with the blood of its neighbors."[64c]

✓ ✓ ✓

"There is nothing more fallacious than to judge the meaning of a philosophic doctrine or the work of a thinker, while ignoring the intellectual medium in which he appears, the militant ends which he pursues, or the political interests which he serves."

So reads the preface to *Philosophic Culture in Spain*,[65] a series of lectures delivered in 1916 at the University of Buenos Aires, in which Ingenieros summarizes rather sketchily the trajectory of Spanish thought from medieval to modern times. What is important to note here is Ingenieros' contention that a study of the history of philosophy is important only to the extent that it teaches us to uncover false metaphysical problems and to avoid illegitimate hypotheses, i.e., errors no longer tolerable in our modern era. Philosophers will no longer inspire unfounded beliefs and superstitions in the same way, for example, that the legendary Cid spread fear as he continued to gallop among his enemies long after he had died.[66]

The above quotation which stresses political-philosophical parallelism is worthy of note, principally in connection with Ingenieros' study of Emile Boutroux (1845-1921). In fact, it is quoted again as part of the text.[67] It is by means of this study that Ingenieros tries to show the relationship between the ideas and attitudes of Boutroux, the historian, and the intellectual currents both within and outside of the University. Boutroux remained a faithful representative of the official University-sponsored philosophy, and reflected its vicissitudes in the course of the turbulent half century, during which time he taught at the École Normale and at the Sorbonne.

The work begins with a description of the philosophical climate in which Boutroux was nurtured. On the eve of Boutroux's birth, the official philosophic doctrine in force at the University was Cousin's eclecticism. This was opposed, on the one hand, by the Catholics who claimed it was pantheistic, irreligious and irrationalist, and on the other hand by the Saint-Simonians of the left (chiefly Republicans and liberal Monarchists) who accused it of hypocrisy, and who were drawn to the banner of Comtism.

By the middle of the century eclecticism was on the decline. The political picture stamped its imprint upon the then reigning ideological strife. For example, since official liberalism aligned itself with scientific Positivism, the Catholic segment resisted it. In the period of the Second Empire, the core of philosophical disputation centered around the age old problem of freedom versus determinism. The Republicans, quite understandably, took the position that to accept determinism implied resigning oneself to the political regime in force. It was therefore not only necessary but also indispensable to stress free will as an instrument of social action. "They were advocates of philosophic freedom because they were fighting for political freedoms."[68]

In the critical period following the Franco-Prussian War and the events of the Paris Commune, French philosophers —following Ingenieros' blueprint—divided into opposing political camps and adjusted their philosophic thinking accordingly. The philosophers attached to the University, whom Ingenieros labels the "philosophical bureaucracy," were all eclectics or "spiritualists, and politically, conservative Monarchists."[69] Wielding greater influence, were the philosophers outside the University who were almost all Republican, anti-clerical and Positivist.

One is treated to a rather curious phenomenon in the philosophical realm—actually an about-face—due to the changing political picture. Whereas under the Second Empire, the Republicans had been advocates of freedom, as

53

opposed to determinism, the Second Republic now witnessed an affirmation and defense of free will against determinism, made by precisely those sectors who were opposed to the Republic. It was this University sector, according to Ingenieros, that was mounting the ramparts against the Republic in the name of God and King, tradition and religion, free will and faith.[70] The "moral order," as opposed to the Republican order, had to be reestablished! At the same time, it was necessary to reaffirm "the sane principles of spiritualism and combat the lamentable aberration of scientific Positivism."[71]

For this purpose, Boutroux was mustered into service. Boutroux's thesis is clear: necessity is not iron-clad, contingency is possible, determinism does not operate in all of nature, and freedom is something which originates in and emanates from God. Contingency exists in nature; natural laws do not exclude it.[72] Without the intervention of a vital, guiding principle, inert matter would not suffice to explain the existence of animate beings. All animate objects, and man in particular, gain in contingency and are less subject to laws of determinism, as they ascend to higher realms of reality. For Boutroux, these realms, in order of ascendency, are: the mathematical, the physical, the animate and the spiritual. And as one ascends from one order to the next, the forces of necessity and determinism diminish, and those of contingency and chance increase. Natural laws become more flexible and creative freedom acquires greater importance.

The laws of nature, formulated by science, are relative and do not imply absolute knowledge of the essence of things. The latter can be attained by the human spirit only via moral and esthetic laws which lead to communion with God. And Boutroux concludes: "free will exists, the soul exists, God exists."[73] Boutroux, affirms Ingenieros, was applauded by the official University circles as well as by reactionary elements who were working against the successful establishment of the Republic.[74]

As the decades wore on, the battle lines were being

stretched taut. Ideological warfare transcended the political boundaries of France. At the close of the century, two large political groups, each with its various sub-groups, crystallized gradually: the leftists who had favored developments in the world of science, and the rightists who had done everything possible to resist scientific advance. Political radicalism, naturalism in literature, and philosophic Positivism had converged. The opposition counter-attacked, equating science with naturalism, and secular education with immorality and social breakdown.

What was Boutroux's mission at this historical juncture? That of aiding the forces of organized religion to stage a comeback. Surely there must be an area of human existence which science could not penetrate or even hope to reach. The separation of church and state as well as the Dreyfus trial had split France into two warring camps. Perhaps a reconciliation between the two opposing ideological currents could be effected. Perhaps it was possible to seek areas of agreement in the terrain of moral and religious values by encouraging the formation of a conservative group within the *Republican* ranks, a group which would endeavor to insure peace and harmony by resisting the excesses of anti-clericalism and the leftism of the socialists.

To this task Boutroux now dedicated himself. Political reconciliation had to be based on philosophical reconciliation. And Boutroux, now recognized as the leading spokesman for the official University philosophic point of view, published his *Science and Religion* (1908), in which, according to Ingenieros, he utilized a mystical approach in order to arrive at a social and moral pantheism.

Scientific reason, argued Boutroux, does not constitute all of human reason. What does this imply? asks Ingenieros. Quite simply: "What is knowable exceeds scientific knowledge; there are means of cognition other than the scientific."[75] The implication is clear: the scientific temper and the religious spirit can co-exist: each serves a different purpose, each operates within a different realm.

Faith, ideal, love: these are three conditions of human

55

action which constitute the basis of the religious spirit. But Ingenieros objects at this point. Faith, ideal and love comprise morality, he asserts, not religion. Boutroux's formulation would not be acceptable "to a Catholic priest, a Protestant minister or a Jewish rabbi."[76] Boutroux has reduced science to the status of relativity and religion to that of ethics. In this sense, they each have sufficient vitality to continue to coexist and grow. Ingenieros maintains that when Boutroux uses the term "religion" as a synonym for mysticism and moral pantheism, he is guilty of philosophical hyprocrisy. It has already been pointed out that Ingenieros' passionate tone leads him, at times, to indulge in characterizations which are somewhat disconcerting to the reader. Another instance of his flair for immoderate language is found in the footnote which follows the charge of philosophical hypocrisy. Ingenieros refers to sophists who believe that it is useful to speak of religion "in order that those who are poor in spirit continue to believe in the superstitions which are the object of the former's scorn. This is another cause of political immorality, of complicity in falsehood."[77]

Ingenieros sees in Boutroux a symbol of the new policy of attempted reconciliation between the French Republic and the Catholic Church—a policy which in Ingenieros' eyes can lead only to a weakening of the Republic. Even though the political segment representing Catholic thought did not agree with Boutroux's mystical tendencies—considering intuitionism and mysticism as expressions of philosophical heresy opposed to the only true philosophy of Thomism[78]—the Church nevertheless utilized Boutroux's contributions in its struggle against its ideological enemies.

To sum up: What is the central issue revealed in Ingenieros' treatise on Boutroux? Ingenieros' anticlerical position leads him to formulate, it would seem, an untenable premise, namely, that a religiously oriented philosophy must necessarily lead to or go hand in hand with political conservatism. Yet this is too convenient an oversimplification. For it is possible to have diverse and even contradictory philosophical positions represented in the same political camp; it is equally true that adherents of the same philosophical orientation may find themselves involved in differing political alignments.

✓ ✓ ✓

In *Toward a Morality without Dogma* and *The Moral Forces*, Ingenieros develops at greater length the question of morality, touched upon briefly in his *Propositions*. Morality is nothing more than experience which is dynamic, and which is "learned by imitation and taught by example."[79] It is legislated and codified conduct adhered to by individuals within a social context, a context characterized by constantly changing social relations. True moral idealism, then, is not metaphysical or theological, but the result of the efforts of those who apply scientific norms to the march of events, in the hope of improving and perfecting the stature, dignity, and solidarity of the members of human society. Idealists are those who strive continually to convert an imperfect present into a better future.

The evolutionary basis of morality is quite clear: morality involves an attitude, rather than a set of preconceived *a priori*, immutable principles; an attitude which seeks to adjust and harmonize to the optimum degree the obligations of the individual and society's respect for his rights.

Religious beliefs, themselves a product of man's culture, undergo transformation in an attempt to insure social cohesion. Religious dogma falls short of attaining ethical values if it has to depend upon supernatural bases. Morality varies in inverse proportion to superstition. It is effective only within a framework of the human and the natural.[80]

In the face of older world religions which have tended to become institutionalized and have acquired a power structure, pure religious emotion has always sought to cleanse established bodies of their *externalia*, giving rise to heretical movements. Awe and wonderment in the presence of the unknown, religious sentiment and poetic emotion, the desire for moral perfection—all of these have always resulted in the yearning for a love of justice, beauty and truth, so that men may lead a better life.

Moral relationships are forged in the give-and-take of daily behavior, especially as a function of man's labor. The right to life itself is conditioned by man's obligation to contribute to society by the dignity of his labor. Productive activity is the key to the emancipation of his personality. Everything that humanity can be proud of is the fruit of man's labor. "All of humanity's capital is accumulated labor."[81]

In 1905 Ingenieros left for Europe to represent his country at an international conference on psychology. Six years later he was to leave again—this time as a protest against what he considered an affront to his dignity and stature as a scholar. One of three candidates for a vacancy in the School of Medicine at the University of Buenos Aires, he had been passed over by the President of the republic, and the appointment given to another contender.

It was on this occasion, during his stay in Switzerland, that he wrote *El hombre mediocre*.[82] Rousseau's second centenary was being celebrated, and as though he had caught the contagion from that incorrigible romantic, he felt inspired to produce some of the most lyrical and vibrant pages of his career.

The appearance of *The Mediocre Man* in 1913 served as a clarion call to the youth of the continent. Its idealistic spirit, breathing optimism as vigorously as it condemned mediocrity, won for its author the enthusiastic acclaim of university youth. His message bore fruit a few years later. Although not the only factor—there were other, deep-seated causes—*The Mediocre Man* may be said to have acted as a catalytic agent for the events which followed. In 1918 the students at the University of Cordoba, Argentina, proclaimed what has since come to be known as a *cause célèbre* in Latin America, namely, the University Reform. Essentially a protest against outworn methods of teaching, inadequate curricular offerings and inefficient administrative organization, the movement soon spread to the entire continent, and merged with social and political rebellion.

A strange assortment of demands is to be found in the various student proclamations and documents, as one examines the development of the reform movement. These reveal the dissatisfaction, characteristic of idealistic youth at a moment when World War I had just come to a close. Aside from agitation for reform programs of a purely university nature, such as the introduction of new courses, improved methods of teaching old courses, the right to choose professors, and student representation in university administration, there were also expressions of admiration for Wilsonian idealism, support of the Bolshevik Revolution, the need for university extension courses for adults, sympathy for the exploited Indian population, protest against "imperialism" in Latin America, and identification with the day-to-day struggles of the laboring classes.*

For understandable reasons, Ingenieros was ignored by the conservative press. He was *persona non grata* in certain circles. Nevertheless, his commentaries filled the pages of journals dedicated to the problems of university youth of the entire Latin American continent. His prestige among these groups was not only undeniable; it was overwhelming. Perhaps he appealed to the youth of the continent to such a great extent, because he, himself, was so very much in love with life, and viewed it in terms of youth and militancy. He always tried to appear youthful and bursting with energy; he feared old age more than death.

The Mediocre Man was perhaps his most readable and, therefore, his most popular work. In it he speaks scathingly of those who place the greatest emphasis upon the immediate, to the exclusion of the ideal. He is in love with the ideal of perfection, dreamed of by great men, and strives to infect Latin American youth with his passionate devotion to this ideal. Perhaps this is why he castigates those without ideals, those who are content to be docile and pas-

---

*For a discussion of the University Reform, see Gabriel del Mazo, *La reforma universitaria*, Buenos Aires, 1927.

sive, those who tear down everything that is outstanding. The "mediocre man," a precursor to Ortega y Gasset's "mass-man," depends upon habit and routine, and deters others from striving toward greater moral improvement. The mediocre individual is an obstacle to creativity; he is incapable of conceiving the idea of perfection, the formation of an ideal. True mediocrity is the custodian of stability; the great mass insures the preservation and continuity of that which is, of what Ingenieros calls the "social personality." The superior individual, on the other hand, rather than being content to imitate, creates and invents, and forges the individual personality; he introduces differences and variations. The morality of the future is a result of individual, rather than collective effort.

The creation of variations and differences, of superiorities and inadequacies, fits neatly into the general framework of the doctrine of natural selection; nature is opposed to a leveling off of all characteristics; sameness and equality would result in stagnation, if not extinction. Evolution depends on the selection of variables. Ingenieros thus connects in masterful fashion, evolutionary doctrine with moral idealism.

In *The Mediocre Man,* he attacks with characteristic impetuosity all obstacles that stand in the way of idealism, an idealism based on experience. Ingenieros repeats here what he has already told us in his *Propositions*: ideals are projections which anticipate experience, and which are created by intelligent imagination. They are visions which are instrumental in the furthering of progress.[83] Experience determines the validity of ideals. However, this does not mean that one must be a slave to the immediate and the practical. Nor is idealism the exclusive property of the spiritualists.[84] Philosophical materialists can be idealists too.

True idealists resist the leveling off, aimed at by the forces of mediocrity.[85] The latter would reduce everyone to the level of the lowest common denominator. Social perfection cannot come about as a result of uniformity. Nature itself has created inequalities. Those who are opposed to

60

differentiation are also against progress; they abhor originality.

Personality depends on differentiation. Variations acquired in the course of experience define an individual as a differentiated personality. To be different is to be someone. The mediocre is characterized by routine patience and imitation; the superior is creatively impatient. Future morality is the result of individual striving, efforts by superior beings who conceive of and endeavor to put into practice goals which are unattainable by the average man.

If a continuous reduction to sameness were possible, if superiority and inferiority were somehow prevented from developing, then humanity would cease to exist. No one is equal in talent to anyone else. It is a mistake to equate democracy with sameness and mediocrity. The greatest theoreticians of the democratic ideal have been those who believe in the doctrine of natural selection. There is nothing wrong with aristocracy, provided it is aristocracy of merit rather than that of caste.[86]

One of the few Americans admired greatly by Ingenieros was Ralph Waldo Emerson. Perhaps it was because he considered Emerson a "heretic," and, therefore, according to his formula, a superior human being, that he devoted so much space to him in his *Toward a Morality without Dogma*. For Emerson represented the possibility of morality without dogmatic sanctions, imposed by religious institutions. What attracted Ingenieros was his belief that the churches in the United States considered moral conduct to be of greater importance than theological principles.

Dogmatism and traditionalism represented paralysis for both Emerson and Ingenieros. Dogma was the equivalent of opinion imposed by authority. Have twenty centuries of Christian dogma resulted in an increase of human kindness? Has moral progress kept pace with material advances? Both Emerson and Ingenieros would respond in the negative. The two were kindred spirits. Both believed that the role of the heretic in history is a salutary one. He who would be a man must be a non-conformist. That is Ingenieros' "superior" man who rises above mediocrity and routine, who places dignity above servility, and virtue above hypocrisy. Heresy is simply that which questions dogma. Socrates, Jesus, Luther, Spinoza—all of these were heretics, and thanks to them, the religious and moral experience of the human race has been enriched. There will always be new heresies as a result of which the moral and religious experience of man will undergo continual transformation.[87]

Development of human personality, inevitable perfectibility, individual rebellion against institutionalized coercion—these are the outstanding themes. Believe in yourself! Confidence in God has been replaced by confidence in oneself.[88] Revolt against social conventionality brings man closer to divinity. Nature, morality and divinity tend to become synonyms. Our morality will be elevated to the extent that we return to the sources of nature; in so doing, we partake of the divine. Emerson shies away from any suggestion of the supernatural. Dogmas tend to interpose themselves between the human spirit and the divine, and with mystical fervor he justifies his opposition to them. But not only theological dogma incurs his displeasure. One must also fight against all other routine: social, political and economic.

Morality, then, which consists of social obligations and sanctions, is rooted in social relationships. The application of scientific methodology—not dogma—to human experience will prevent future opinions from hardening into dogma. This experiential approach to the formulation of ethical guidelines once again completes the circle. We are back at the "metaphysics of experience." In applying this experiential yardstick to the structuring of human behavior, we will have arrived at a morality without dogma.

Emerson represents a step forward in this development: morality is human and natural, and does not depend on a supernatural framework involving life after death. The unitarianism and transcendentalism of his day constitute an effort in the direction of reducing the dependence of morality upon dogma. Moreover, for Emerson, the romantic reformer, evil does not exist as a positive entity in its own right. Evil is simply the absence of good. Emerson, the transcendentalist, always appeals to emotion rather than logic. He resorts to imagery and sentiment, not ordered and coherent structure. He is therefore more of an inspired, mystical prophet than a systematic philosopher.

One may well ask at this point: is there not a contradiction in the fact that, on the one hand, Ingenieros praises the non-conformist, the heretic, the superior man who is different, and on the other, he advocates a system of ethics that aspires to human solidarity and harmony? Furthermore, is it possible for man to live the good life according to the highest moral standards, without resorting to dogmatic imperatives, and in complete absence of supernatural sanctions? At the same time, does not Ingenieros' insistence on the "experiential" and the "scientific," create a new type of dogma? For science, too, is based on hypotheses and postulates, and postulates can be dogmas.

Ingenieros would probably reply that when one speaks of a future morality without dogma, one must bear in mind not only religious dogma; what is also implied is rational dogma.[89] Both theological and rational dogma set themselves up as unchangeable in space and time and are, therefore, inimical to the truth. It is equally absurd to speak in terms of a definitive, scientific philosophy, a scientific dogmatism, since science itself is always unfinished. A scientific philosophy is simply a body of systems of hypotheses utilized to explain problems which transcend present and future experience, said hypotheses being based upon scientifically proven laws. These hypotheses will engage in a constant interaction with experience; both will rectify each other incessantly.

Basically, the problem should be stated as follows: How can a morality based on experience reconcile satisfactorily individual rights and social duties? All societies, he maintains, have in the course of their evolution undergone changes in moral codes as a result of variations of social experience. Basing oneself upon this point of view, it is but a short step to take if one wishes to postulate that the study

63

of all moral experiences is nothing more than an historical account of customs and manners.[90]

Morality, then, can develop and flourish without having to be dependent upon supernatural elements. What is moral is natural, human and independent of metaphysical speculation and religious dogma. If men would only place their faith in this type of orientation, then the conflict between science and religion would disappear. Ingenieros hopes, too, that if this were the case, churches would evolve toward a position that would accept and advocate, not a morality *without* dogma—Ingenieros is not *that* naive—but at least a morality with *less* dogma. He nevertheless admits that dogma has the positive value of insuring the cohesiveness of the social group. One may well ask in this connection: How many individuals have the capacity for leading a virtuous life without having to depend upon religious dogma for their moral sustenance?

The individual who abandons his religious dogmas would be obliged to strengthen his practical morality.[91] Social sanctions are as severe as divine or rational sanctions. In this connection, Ingenieros puts much stock in the power of formal education. Only with the aid of the school will humanity march forward toward a morality without dogma. Dogmas divide men; the moral ideal unites them.

One can only say in conclusion that in spite of the unabashed, youthful enthusiasm of Ingenieros, the obvious weakness in his position is simply the fact that he seems to have substituted one dogma for another. He has set forth hypotheses which might themselves conceivably develop into dogmas. Again one asks at this point: How is it possible to develop within men a feeling of solidarity and harmony when the very premises of the doctrine which is being advanced are based on a policy of non-conformism and rebellion?

Upon looking at the man, Ingenieros—at the whole man—after having examined his voluminous contributions, one is struck in retrospect by the apparent contradiction revealed by this multifaceted personality. On the one hand, one recalls the careful, systematic, scientific approach and treatment in his works dealing with psychology and sociology; on the other, one is swept away by the bold, impetuous, almost lyrical qualities of his writing in the field of ethics. In Ingenieros, the scientist: innumerable details, laboriously elaborated and explained—all structured and joined together in painstaking fashion until they form a colossal edifice. By contrast, in Ingenieros, the poet: impassioned accusations, hurled like thunderbolts against ideological opponents, imaginative visions and daring hypotheses, soaring metaphors and richly-colored word pictures. Hard-headed scientist versus incorrigible romantic. Ingenieros had room for both; the one did not seem to disturb the other.

CHAPTER THREE

Alejandro Korn

POSITIVISM, NATURALISM and Darwinism could not expect to continue to dominate the philosophic scene in Argentina. As World War I drew to a close, new philosophic currents which had arrived earlier from abroad began to grow in strength and vigor. Bergson's "creative evolution," the rebirth of Kant's idealism,* and neo-Thomism—all of these threatened to replace the mechanistic-deterministic oriented tendencies which had been in vogue for forty years. Coriolano Alberini inaugurated a course in Kantian idealism and one on Bergsonian intuitionism at the University of Buenos Aires. The situation was ripe for the appearance of Argentina's foremost non-positivist. Alejandro Korn substituted for the depersonalizing effects of biological determinism the rights of the human personality and the importance of spiritual values.

Korn was the last representative of the generation of 1880[1] (in the intellectual sense)—that group which, as has already been pointed out, exercised a decisive influence on the economic and cultural development of Argentina. Yet it can be said that he went beyond its positivist-oriented strictures. Schopenhauer awakened in him an interest in speculation, in metaphysical and religious concern. He delved into the works of the mystics, oriental as well as European. He was familiar with Ortega, Bergson, Dilthey and Scheler, to mention but a few representatives of the newer philosophic currents which were reaching the continent. This in

---

* The Kantian Society of Buenos Aires was founded in 1929.

66

itself can be said to have been indicative of an expanding philosophic horizon in Latin America generally, and Argentina in particular. The philosophic enterprise was no longer the uniform monopoly of a given school. Intellectual fermentation was the outgrowth of democratic advances in the political arena. New social and economic sectors of the population were making their appearance. This was especially true of a growing urban middle class which was winning for itself increasing access to cultural pursuits.

Korn had come to philosophy from medicine. Yet he was not only a philosopher. He was a man of deep social convictions who always felt that, as a citizen, he should not confine his energies exclusively to the classroom. Perhaps this is why, in his later years, he joined the Socialist Party, a move motivated by strong ethical considerations and dictated by the rather murky political situation, resulting from the Uriburu dictatorship of 1930. It is also interesting to note in this connection, that the royalties obtained from the publication of his *Apuntes filosóficos* were turned over to the Socialist Party.[1a] Not only did he fail to profit financially from any of his works; he contributed with his own resources to the programs of many cultural institutions, such as the *Colegio Libre de Estudios Superiores de Buenos Aires* which he helped found.

Korn was also associated with the University Reform movement.* He was the first dean of the School of Philosophy and Letters of the University of Buenos Aires, elected with the participation of the students. He was involved in student activities at the University of La Plata, where his influence was even more lasting. Korn was one of the few professors who sympathized with the agitation that characterized the student revolt; he knew well the underlying causes which led to the eruption. It was necessary at times, he asserted, to break a few windows in order to allow some fresh air to come in.

It was always Korn's belief that philosophy could not be

---

* See pages 58-59.

divorced from historic reality. One thinks immediately of Alberdi upon reading the following: "A philosophy divorced from reality, a new university philosophy, word play and abstract digressions—all this runs counter to our national temper."[1b] It is within its own social and cultural milieu that Argentina must seek and find the solutions to its problems.

Korn makes his appearance upon the philosophic scene as a "subjectivistic or voluntaristic idealist," and as a philosopher of relativist value in the historicist or pragmatic tradition.[1c] In Korn, Argentine philosophy comes of age. Korn was averse to wholesale importation of European philosophic formulas in uncritical, mechanical fashion. He would maintain contact with European thought, but he preferred to see therein a point of departure to be utilized for the exploration and solution of Argentine problems.

Korn's principal objective seems to have been to have man reach out and go beyond philosophical materialism and scientific determinism which make of him a mere plaything and deprive him of his dignity.

For Korn, the solution to all contemporary problems (and the world itself is a problem) is to be found in an ethical principle, a principle which speaks in terms of obligations, responsibilities, sanctions, and above all, freedom. "The new philosophy," he writes, "has to return to us the dignity of our free and conscious personality, master of its destiny... If we want a better world, we will create it."[2]

The reaction to positivism and scientific determinism is illustrative of the periodic oscillations of the philosophic pendulum. Positivism and "scientism" were themselves reactions: reactions to the unbridled ambitions of an all-encompassing German idealism, as typified by Hegel, Fichte, and Schelling. In a similar manner, when positivism overreached itself Europe witnessed a return to Kant. Research in epistemological problems assumed primary importance.

Korn's philosophy is one which stresses personality, freedom, value. He is therefore opposed to a deterministic naturalism which conceives of a universe governed by blind, mechanical forces. Man, far from being submerged by this naturalistic world, rises above it, *creates* it via his cognitive powers and manages thereby to remain apart therefrom.

The field of knowledge, according to Korn, is shared by both science and philosophy. Science interprets objective reality mathematically, i.e., in a quantitative sense. Objective reality is reality which is external to us. Science judges the world of space, i.e., all that takes place within space and can be measured. However, the function of science is not merely to compile empirical data, but to furnish an interpretation thereof, to record relationships between various phenomena. On the other hand, philosophy concerns itself with the subject which functions within this objective reality. The subject reacts to this reality and evaluates it continually. He does so positively and negatively. The realm of the subjective, then, must perforce deal with problems of value. Values are renewed and modified; each generation forges its own.

Science can never hope to give us a complete description of external reality, nor can it ever penetrate the very essence thereof. What it can do, however, is to provide us with the means of effective action. Korn, then, does not admit the absolute quality of scientific knowledge. At best, scientific induction can only yield probable results, relative truths, which are subject to correction. Scientific hypotheses are utilized as long as they are pragmatically sound. Once they prove untenable, they are cast aside. Yet science remains the outstanding creation of man's intelligence.

Positivism did not realize the distinction between objective reality, the domain of science, and subjective attitudes, the concern of philosophy. It tried to attribute a scientific basis to every human problem. It ignored the fundamental duality between subject and object, two terms which are incapable of being welded together as one.[3]

✓ ✓ ✓

Has the world turned more charitable, is there more justice, has humanity improved, as a result of scientific progress? asks Korn. The obvious answer in the negative is the result of having tried to apply a unifying principle to the world and its phenomena, when in reality there are two separate and distinct worlds: the outer world of nature and the inner one of consciousness. In Korn's judgment, the external or objective world obeys necessary laws and is predictable and deterministic, whereas the inner, subjective realm is free and autonomous.

One cannot, as the Positivists tried to do, subject the free, subjective world of the person to a rigid determinist automatism. The present crisis of spiritual values is precisely a by-product of this mechanist-scientific approach. All ethical, esthetic and religious values, maintains Korn, have been subsumed under material norms, and are being strangled by the economic octopus.

Man is free, but not omnipotent. His will power impels him forward to action, but in the process he encounters obstacles within the outer world of nature, as well as within himself, i.e., his impulses and passions.

Man will achieve a greater measure of freedom to the degree that he succeeds in dominating both worlds: the outer and the inner. In mastering the external, natural realm he will attain economic freedom; to the extent that he achieves mastery over himself, he will achieve moral freedom. Both are necessary; each complements the other. The final product will be human freedom.

This condition, however, is not reached via the road of passive contemplation, but rather through creative and rebellious activity. Man is a rebelling animal. It is not the struggle for existence that is of primary importance, but rather the struggle to achieve the type of human freedom which Korn formulates, a freedom which is the measure of personal dignity.

Human responsibility is impossible if man's behavior is determined by biological factors or by any other rigidly conditioning elements. It then becomes futile to speak of ethics. Man, in Korn's view, is equivalent to the exercise of freedom. Man creates culture and writes history.

Freedom, then, is the very essence of man. He needs it

in order to control, improve and create. Freedom is creative. This is Korn's principal theme which he advances as the basis for a theory of values.

✓ ✓ ✓

Korn, as an advocate of creative freedom, is interested in tracing the history of the conflict between science and philosophy, the background of which explains the growth of Positivism in his native land. Originally, he maintains, philosophy embraced all branches of knowledge. It denied the existence of a separate role and field of investigation for science. But beginning with the 17th century, scientific investigation, utilizing methods and techniques peculiar unto itself, explored the empirical world, gaining in vigor as it progressed, and ended by freeing itself completely from the influence of philosophical speculation. This process reached its apex in the second half of the 19th century, when the roles were found to be reversed. Science now claimed to hold the key to the solution of all problems. Philosophy was reduced to a subsidiary role. The exaggerated confidence demonstrated by science was transferred to the adherents of Positivism, who reduced all social phenomena to mathematical formulae. The universe was converted into a rigid mechanism, governed by quantitative relationships; no opportunity was provided for the exercise of a free act. Human personality was completely swallowed up by an absolute automatism.[4] Yet the rule of necessity, protests Korn, which supposedly governs the totality of the cosmos, does not apply to that which cannot be measured. Only that which is spatial can be subjected to mathematical coercion. Only the realm of objects is ruled by mechanical necessity. The realm of the subjective, the activity of the subject which develops in time, not in space, rebels against this control. It aspires to dominate, rather than to be dominated. This aspiration is called freedom.[5]

Such is the origin of the reaction against Positivism. Human personality must be rehabilitated, its intrinsic dignity salvaged; man must once again resume responsibility for his actions. This is not to deny or diminish the author-

71

ity of science. It is merely a question of delimiting its area. The attempt to reduce psychology, sociology and history to the level of exact sciences has not succeeded.

The problem, then is "to overcome the pseudo-scientific conception of mechanical determinism and to salvage the rights of human personality within the limits of experience without resorting in the 20th century to metaphysical fiction or archaic mythology."[6] It is a distortion of the facts to equate historical movements with the natural process or to compare the development of culture with that of nature.

The anti-positivist reaction, according to Korn, is characterized by an upsurge in metaphysical speculation as well as a revival of religious sentiment. In the case of the unsophisticated masses, who likewise experience this metaphysical need, there has been a return to the old dogmas and outworn rituals, for the simple reason that nothing effective has arisen to take their place.

The revival of religion and the renewed interest in metaphysics, characteristic of the close of the 19th century and the beginning of the 20th, have their counterpart in art and literature. The latter are likewise reacting to disorientation, restlessness and anarchy, and are characterized by a certain degree of anguish, misfortune, tragedy and fear of cataclysm. These are the characteristic notes of the times which give rise to tense emotional reactions in literature, philosophy and religion. Only in this way can one explain the "metaphysical regression," a phenomenon which may well be called neo-romantic, because of its resemblance to the movement which erupted in the 18th and the beginning of the 19th centuries as a reaction against the intellectualism of the period. Of course, there are important differences: the present neo-romantic "metaphysical regression" appears subsequent to the impressive progress made by science. However, in each case there is an emphasis on impulse and sentiment, on religious exaltation, on vital forces, as opposed to logical and intellectual orientation.

Korn, like the Positivists he criticized, utilized all available data. However, he considered it perfectly legitimate to investigate the preconditions under which these data were made possible, e.g., space, time and consciousness. In this respect he went beyond Positivist doctrine. Furthermore, Korn did not subscribe to the three Comtian stages of development nor to the Spencerian law of evolution. For him, religion was a constant factor, ever-present in the course of humanity's progress. Philosophy was not, as it had been for Comte, a positive science. Scientific methodology and philosophic reflection were not equivalent. He could therefore not admit the existence of natural laws, simultaneously valid for the physical world as well as for the spiritual realm, as Comte believed.[7]

Whereas Comte had rejected the difference between phenomenon and noumenon, Korn admitted the possibility of a being underlying all phenomena. He made a distinction between the *modus cognoscendi* and the *modus essendi;* our knowledge was limited to the *modus cognoscendi.* Just because empirical investigation could not penetrate the realm of noumena, did not necessarily mean that this realm did not exist.

Nor did Korn agree with Spencer concerning the latter's belief that the measure of science was to prove the all-encompassing nature of the law of evolution. Not all problems pertaining to man could be solved scientifically. Rejecting the rigid determinism which had figured so prominently in the thinking of Ingenieros, Korn upheld individual liberty and free will. He saw in utilitarian morality a threat to spiritual values, although he did agree with John Stuart Mill that experience was the only source of knowledge.

Positivism flourished in Argentina simply because of a favorable climate. Historical circumstances dictated an aversion toward speculation and a lack of sensitivity in religious matters. The economic development of the country was paramount; hence, morality was affected and conditioned by a utilitarian mentality. Positivism just happened to coincide with the needs of Argentina and consequently, furnished the necessary ideology required to justify and fortify a policy of commercial expansionism. It was not possessed of a methodically developed philosophic structure. Its narrowness provided Korn with a target against which he aimed his sharpest darts.

Korn believed that the new philosophic currents of the 20th century had gone beyond the type of thinking to which the empirical sciences had given prestige and popularity. Nature's laws were no longer to be considered as absolutely unchangeable. The problem of man's freedom was assuming primary proportions. A socially positive system of ethics made its appearance, one which stressed the value of personality and the dignity of human effort in the face of life's risks and dangers.

After the death of Hegel, the metaphysical systems of German idealism which had held exalted sway appeared to give way to a greater concern for immediate problems. The second half of the century was characterized by an avoidance of abstract speculation. The sciences of the spirit were "subjected to the methods of the natural sciences."[8] The older disciplines became fragmented; various branches of knowledge were subdivided and compartmentalized. Psychology, e.g., developed into an empirical science and then became experimental. This was the age of Positivist thinking. Metaphysics and mythology were "obstacles in the way of progress . . ."[9] English agnosticism asserted its affinity for an empiricism which it linked with evolutionary doctrine. German thought, under the influence of Kant, was convinced that the noumenon is quite inaccessible and that only the world of phenomena is the proper object of knowledge. The period was further characterized by the attempt to explain all physical and psychic phenomena in terms of a mechanical law, universally applicable.

But a reaction was bound to set in. At the close of the century, the very men who were steeped in Positivist doctrine realized the inadequacy of the structure within which they had been operating. They began to deal with supra-empirical concepts which no longer lent themselves to tangible proof, thereby indulging in metaphysics. The barrier standing in the way of the "unknowable" had been swept

74

away, a barrier so dear to Positivism. Substance was now conceived of as pure activity; the universe was one endless process of becoming. The principle of evolution had apparently struck deep roots, a principle that could be applied to everything under investigation. Truth, value, freedom—these did not exist, they *became*. This active principle was called energy by the realists. Their mechanistic interpretation spoke in terms of a universal law which dictates a pre-determined process. On the other hand, the vitalists were striving to make room in this scheme of things for the principle of freedom; they were interested in ethical rather than scientific concepts. And Korn concludes: "There can be no science if contingency is admitted; there can be no ethics where implacable necessity reigns."[10]

✓   ✓   ✓

In his discussion of contemporary philosophic movements, Korn establishes some interesting contrasts. Romantic philosophy, e.g., had been completely divorced from empirical research: it aspired to know reality via the intuitive process. Present-day philosophy, by contrast, far from losing its contact with the experimental sciences, depends on them for its effective functioning. "Today we do not have philosophers who attempt to create natural science, but rather naturalists who make metaphysics."[11]

Romanticism was essentially pessimistic, as reflected in the works of its literary exponents, e.g., Byron, Leopardi, Poe, and, philosophically, in Schopenhauer. It involved a backward-looking orientation toward a utopia situated in bygone times; the present was generally looked down upon. On the other hand, the philosopher of the present bases his ethical configuration on an affirmative, although not naively optimistic orientation. His is a view that seeks sustenance in life, energy and will-power. Fully conscious of the negative aspects of our existence, he nevertheless calls upon us to face up to them, to lend dignity to our actions in spite of them, and to build a better world in accord with the ideals which he envisions.

This positive approach separates us from the visionary

75

romantic and makes us resemble more the man of the Renaissance. The former was ineffective as concerns programs of action; the latter had more than his share of bold initiative, was overbubbling with energy, and was continually avid for new adventures. One may conceivably express mild surprise at this point. Korn's own countrymen headed by Esteban Echeverría, who was himself inspired by the Romantic tradition, can certainly not be accused of intellectual sterility insofar as their militant opposition to the Rosas tyrannical regime is concerned. Yet there is a further distinction to be made between the age of the Renaissance man and our own. The former "was an age of great individualities; ours is one of great collective movements."[12]

The spirit of individualism found its systematic rationale in John Locke's doctrine which viewed society as an institution designed to protect the natural rights of man, so that he could have the greatest latitude possible to engage in his activities. It was a doctrine adjusted to the secular interests of a growing middle class, culminating in Spencerian liberalism, and one which ultimately demolished the restrictive institutions of the Middle Ages.

Collectivism plus a philosophy which lent it substantiation were bound to appear as a necessary corrective to the abuses of an unbridled individualism. Ethical norms were needed to guide human behavior to a higher level than that of egotistical individualism. This is the historical juncture at which we now find ourselves. Korn maintains that a philosophy of values will provide just such an expression. If in the past we have freed the individual from all restraints in order to further his development, we now need a philosophy which would make him aware of the fact that there are values which are higher than his own individual interests, values which are to be placed within the social context.

Positivism, enmeshed as it was in the coils of a mechanist orientation, had limited ethics to a study of habits and customs. It imagined that science could resolve all problems of human interest. Disillusionment was inevitable: science was

76

only an instrument which could be put to use with equal efficacy for both good and evil.

To what use should our knowledge be put at the present moment? And Korn answers: We must formulate a philosophy of value, an ethic which "must be collectivist, because it represents a legitimate protest against the excesses of the industrial age which degrades man . . "[13] At the same time we must guard against any movement which threatens to oppress man morally, regardless of whether this movement comes from the right or left. The greatest achievement of modern philosophy is the concept of tolerance. It would indeed be tragic if any movement, regressive in nature, were to place this concept in jeopardy.

The new system of values, supreme in essence, will nevertheless be transitory, since humanity, in the course of time, always stands ready to create, eliminate or modify. This is implicit in man's creativity. For let us remember: "The human being is not only action, he is creative action."[14] We would certainly be guilty of the grossest of errors if, on the one hand, we were to affirm the pragmatic and fragmentary nature of our knowledge and then, on the other, try to arrive at a rational solution to our problems, definite for all times.

Furthermore, although Korn criticizes some of the thinking of the past, he refuses to reject it completely, particularly the Argentine past. He would saw off some of the branches, but not the trunk. The development of Argentine thought was linked primarily to the economic factor. Alberdi, with penetrating insight, had arrived at the same conclusions as Marx; yet Alberdi had never known Marx. The philosophic influences of Comte, Spencer and Marx penetrated the Argentine landscape forty years after Alberdi had proposed his solution to the nation's problems. Emphasis on the economic factor was therefore truly native, rather than imported from abroad. It was reinforced by the European brands. Argentine conditions were sufficiently ripe to insure a cordial reception of Comtism and Spencerianism, and a consequent repudiation of metaphysical speculation.

77

Faith in science, indifference to religion—these were the characteristics that marked the intellectual climate of the day. However, scientific truth was bound to lose its absolute hegemony, asserts Korn. Scientific interpretation is subject to continued modification. Mechanistic views of human development called forth a reaction in terms of the dignity of the human personality. Korn is careful as to what he accepts or rejects. He accepts economic conditioning as an intrinsic factor in the evolution of his country. This is "Argentina's creation." He also accepts the reaction to scientific absolutism in making room for human personality. What he rejects is a reaction against science in the form of a complete return to conceptions of the past, such as subjecting oneself to some theological or metaphysical truth, equally absolute.

Positivism has completed its mission—a necessary one—but now we should be careful not to break the continuity of our ideological development. We should now find solutions to present-day problems, and these are our own national problems, not those of other lands; they are not universal problems. In short, economic problems of Argentina should be the concern of any new philosophic system we may wish to select or create. Not to do so is tantamount to divorcing ourselves from the life of our people.[14a] Instead, the early primitive positivism of Alberdi should be transcended, which, in fact, has already been done. An effort should be made to raise to a higher level the economic factor, to place it at the service of and fuse it with ideals of human solidarity. Argentina must go beyond the exclusively material in its ideological evolution.

✦   ✦   ✦

Korn's critique of the development of Positivism in his country is part of a larger, more comprehensive work entitled *Influencias filosóficas en la evolución nacional*. In order to paint an accurate picture of the intellectual climate of Argentina, Korn goes back to the historical situation of the mother country at the time of the Catholic Reformation and presents a panoramic view of the cultural heritage bequeathed unto her daughters. In the chapter entitled "Scholasticism," Korn reviews the dominant trends in theological, political and social thought of the colonial period, the activities of the missionaries, the question of Indian slavery and the scholastic controversies. He concludes that the defect of Scholasticism lay not so much in the fact that its adherents taught badly, but rather in what they failed to teach.[15]

The second part of his *Influencias filosóficas* is devoted to a review of the fresh currents of thought which began to reach the River Plate region in the 17th and 18th centuries: Descartes, Bacon, Locke, the Encyclopedists. Korn discusses the impact upon Argentine life of such political and economic theories as liberalism and mercantilism. The section dealing with Romanticism introduces us to the reaction against the intellectualism of the Encyclopedists. The Rosas dictatorship was an authoritarian, regressive, nationalist movement; anti-liberal, anti-philosophical, in fact, anti-European. But there were other ingredients to be added to the romantic process: Hegelian idealism, socialism, Cousin's eclecticism. These were the days of Alberdi, Sarmiento and Mitre, the luminaries of the intellectual life of the nation, the associates of Echeverría, the Saint-Simonian romantic, who had been responsible for the founding of the *Asociación de Mayo*.

Of the above mentioned group, Alberdi is the chief representative of an "autochthonous" positivism. Although he shared in the active enthusiasm of his revolutionary companions, Alberdi's contact with English utilitarianism and French Encyclopedism prevented him from being completely overwhelmed by the waves of Romanticism. Korn refers to a series of lectures on contemporary philosophers, given by Alberdi, and published in 1842, as being one of the first documents of Argentine Positivism. To prove the point, Korn quotes Alberdi's criticism of Cousin's spiritual eclecticism:[16]

> There is, then, no universal philosophy, because there is no universal solution of questions which constitute its essence. Each country, each age, each point of view, has had its particular philosophy ... In the process of

79

solving basic problems which are of interest to the current existence and destiny of the American people, let us utilize . . . a philosophy for Americans, not one for the Universe . . . Our discussion will limit itself to positive and real philosophy, to a philosophy applied to the political, religious and social interests of these countries, rather than speculative philosophy or philosophy for its own sake . . .[16a]

Thus, Alberdi felt that romantic gyrations were not enough to cope with the pressing problems of his country. Then years later, Alberdi was to write his famous *Bases,* a proposed model of constitutional government to be followed by Argentina. Comte and Spencer were to come later.[17]

Alberdi's "practical" philosophy is further illustrated by his famous dictum: "to govern is to populate." Men and capital have to emigrate from Europe. Old habits must die; new interests must be created. What is of paramount importance is to build the country; the economic motif is primary. Alberdi's position on the freedom of religion is revealing: he does not appeal to freedom of individual conscience as a fundamental human right, as the basis for religious tolerance. Instead, his argument is one of expediency: Argentina needs immigrants, and immigrants may profess different religions. Let us therefore have freedom of worship.[18]

Sarmiento, too, represents a phase of native Argentine Positivism. Sarmiento's conception of civilization is "purely utilitarian and positive."[19] Civilization for Sarmiento is the affirmation of law and constituted authority, the education of the masses at the elementary school level, and the removal of all obstacles in the way of economic growth.

If Alberdi looked to Europe as the proper source for Argentina's salvation, Sarmiento sought and found his inspiration in the United States. It was the great neighbor to the north that inspired him with its enterprising spirit, its technical sense and its system of public education.

Korn then proceeds to discuss the two generations of

Positivists that followed Alberdi and Sarmiento. The first group led the Argentine people to experience its most profound crisis.[20] If the generation of Alberdi and Sarmiento never gave a thought to personal aggrandizement, the generation that followed Caseros at which the dictator Rosas met his Waterloo, entertained no such scruples. A vulgarized, materialistic conception of life became the national norm. For example, higher education was professionalized beyond measure. Any subject unrelated to the immediate necessities of life was unceremoniously dropped from the secondary school curriculum, e.g., classical languages and philosophy. This was the generation that saw in Positivism the confirmation of Alberdi's thinking.

The third generation within the Positivist movement, superior intellectually to its predecessor, sensed the lack of a value system and attempted to erect an organic philosophic base, designed to effect an ethical regeneration of the country. This moral upsurge within the Positivist tradition was to lead to the Revolution of 1890, directed against the "financial oligarchy."[21] It was this group, too, that developed studies in psychology and sociology along the strictly deterministic lines of the natural sciences. Its members shared a profound faith in "the possibility of a political science derived from empirical facts;"[22] they expected experimental psychology to reveal to them significant aspects of the spiritual life of man. The members of this positivist-oriented group were split in two sub-groups: the university-trained disciples of Spencer, and the Normal School nucleus at Paraná, which was influenced largely by Comte.[23]

The Spencerian Positivists of Buenos Aires and Córdoba, in accordance with the evolutionary and agnostic doctrines of the master, enthusiastically accepted the deterministic influences of the natural sciences, the rigorous application of the experimental method to all fields of human inquiry, and finally, the individualism of English liberalism. The University of La Plata, established by Joaquín V. González, was devoted exclusively to scientific research and experimental methods. On the other hand, the Paraná Normal

81

School became the center of Comtism; the concept of order, discipline and method prevailed. Doubt was unknown. Paraná was convinced that it possessed the truth. It had reached "the third Comtian stage, a state of perfect beatitude which does not admit of a greater beyond, nor the existence of anything problematical."[24]

Yet Korn is not too harsh in his judgment. He admits that the Argentine Comtians constituted an excellent corps of teachers, that they initiated the spiritual and economic emancipation of women, and organized the elementary school system of the nation. Korn asks at this point, introducing thereby a problem to which he was to dedicate an entire lifetime: Was a higher type of culture possible if this was to be inspired by Comte and Spencer, the two individuals who, in the entire history of philosophy, were least endowed with esthetic sensitivity? Could one expect an ethical regeneration from a philosophy which denied human personality?[25]

Korn maintains that his generation was excessively immersed in European models and therefore sought foreign remedies for native ills, without perceiving the possibilities inherent in the Argentine landscape. Could one expect a restoration of Argentine ideals, to be effected by those who have been hypnotized by the minutiae of a foreign culture?

Korn's critical-mindedness is next applied to Ingenieros' formulation of a "metaphysics of experience."[26] The very fact, says Korn, that Ingenieros dared to use the term "metaphysics," equating it with philosophy, and asserting that we cannot close our eyes to its necessity is evidence that he realized the inadequacy of a narrowly conceived "scientific" interpretation of all phenomena, characteristic of Argentine Positivism.

If, as Ingenieros maintains, metaphysics is to deal only with those problems which lie beyond human experience, i.e., which cannot be verified via experimentation, it follows that its field of operation will be reduced to the extent that scientific verification makes greater inroads into unsolved problems.

Korn enters a demurrer at this point. He perceives a linguistic difficulty here. Should we not distinguish between the "inexperienced" and the "non-experienced," i.e., between that which has not yet been experienced to date (scientifically or otherwise) and what is perhaps incapable of direct experience? In short, Ingenieros speaks in terms of the "unknown" but not the "unknowable." According to Ingenieros, metaphysics begins where scientific hypotheses can no longer advance. The ideal of science is to reduce the terrain governed by metaphysics. Yet science itself, suggests Korn, may be "infested" with certain metaphysical concepts and assumptions. Perhaps these should be put on the witness stand and subjected to cross-examination.[27]

Moreover, before science can assume the status of a metaphysics with any degree of validity, it is necessary for the various conclusions derived from its diverse branches to achieve some measure of agreement among themselves. The supposed unity of the sciences is a Positivist superstition, a myth of bygone times. In the realm of the experimental, there is neither physical, organic nor psychic unity. Both science and metaphysics are indispensable. Metaphysics is not a continuation or extension of science; each operates in a different realm, each needs the other. Ingenieros maintains that experience is the only source of knowledge. Yet, protests Korn, he never really explains or analyzes what this experience consists of, nor the value or limits of this knowledge.[28] Ingenieros is guilty of oversimplification when he assumes *a priori* that our cognitive powers are limitless.

The problem of freedom, so intimately related to that of the human personality and so fundamental for Korn, occupies as has been indicated, a primary position in the era of post-Positivism. Are all acts rigidly determined by antecedents, or is there room for spontaneity? In the reaction against positivist determinism, Korn cites "one of the most curious attempts"[29] on the part of freedom to assert itself, made by the French philosopher, Boutroux.[30]

Boutroux had attempted to show that even within the

framework of physical nature itself, there exists a certain indeterminism, because not all events can be predicted necessarily. Furthermore, Boutroux maintained that in the realm of organic matter the measure of freedom is increased. This is even more so when one enters the psychic life of human consciousness.

However, the entire problem has to be refocused in view of the changing perspective adopted by modern science. The concept of fixed and unchanging law has been abandoned by physicists. Research into the molecular structure of matter has concluded that rigid determinism is not always applicable; the law is not as absolute as has been supposed. Essentially, it is invalid to "identify phenomena which we attribute to the physical world with phenomena of a psychic world, revealed in our consciousness."[31] There is no point in trying to ascertain whether a stone, in falling, does so freely or not. On the other hand, it is quite to the point to discuss whether man acts freely or not; we all know whether an act committed by us springs from our spontaneous will or whether it has been performed because it could not be otherwise. Admittedly, the issue is not always so simple or clear-cut. It is not a question of either—or. Frequently, if not in the majority of cases, our free will combines with suggestions and impositions which originate either within or outside ourselves.

Moreover, on the level of the empirical, discussion as to the relative degree of freedom is not overly complicated. It is when we go beyond the empirical, and try to discover whether this opposition between freedom and necessity operates in the realm which transcends the experimental and the verifiable, that we run into difficulties and attempt metaphysical solutions. One of these solutions, for example, finds its basis in the existence of an absolute principle, God, which controls both physical and psychic phenomena.

And here Korn repeats his suggestion to the effect that all the difficulties engendered by this antinomy, i.e., between free will and determinism, as well as all other contradictions, are of our own making. We ourselves have created what Korn refers to as dualisms.[31a] For to think is to relate, and we relate in terms of opposites. This polarization, the product of our own psychological mechanism, should not be thought of as having greater reality than that of the empirical world. We create the problem *a posteriori*. In the course of action, emotion or ecstasy, there is no dualism. As we think and reflect the dualism appears. Then we realize that our knowledge is deficient in the face of the relative and the accidental, and so we resort to the principle of the absolute. In short, "we experience the metaphysical need, but we do not have the means available to satisfy it."[32] All great religions have served to satisfy this metaphysical urgency.

Korn's confidence in human reason is limited. It is true, he maintains, that rational treatment of experimental data is the only legitimate road to knowledge. But this road often leads to insoluble contradictions. Instead of being paralyzed in the face of this by a depressing scepticism, we should cut the "Gordian knot" by embarking upon a course of action. History teaches us that action leads us away from doubt and perplexity, and has caused us to rise above our animality, creating culture in the process. Action, then, is simply a way of expressing in concrete fashion our "creative freedom."[33]

✓   ✓   ✓

Insofar as the field of epistemology is concerned, Korn would be classified as an "idealist." Korn criticizes the realistic position by affirming that knowledge is possible only via that which is present in human consciousness.

Science concerns itself with external reality. It does so in the form of mathematics whenever possible, and in theoretical formulations whenever exactitude becomes impossible. Philosophy, on the other hand, is concerned, not with objects but with the subject and his reactions and appraisals. Metaphysics lies outside the field of objective knowledge. It would therefore seem that all metaphysical formulations have meaning and value only for those who create them and believe in them.

Korn, the "first Argentine idealist,"[34] does not accept

85

the realistic position that outside the human consciousness there exists a "duplicate" of the universe. On the contrary space, time and causality, which constitute the world of philosophical realism are for him "but elements of consciousness" (as they are for Kant, upon whom he leans heavily). It is consciousness that makes of objects an ordered cosmos. Knowledge would seem to be limited to consciousness.

And yet Korn does not quite accept, in unqualified fashion, the position of absolute idealism. He combats realism because it is a disguised materialism and therefore a denial of human freedom, especially ethical freedom. In this connection, he makes a sharp distinction between absolute idealism and extreme realism. "In the first case," he writes, "consciousness would be the center of irradiation of the cosmic process, it would be a creative power of its own world conception; in the other case, consciousness would be an accidental efflorescence whose presence or absence would not affect the development of the universal mechanism. In the first case, consciousness would not only be active, but would be the only existing activity. In the second case, it would not only be receptive; it would also be completely passive . . ."[35] In the latter instance, too, freedom becomes impossible; there is no basis for morality, nor for human personality. Therefore, only consciousness exists, but it is a consciousness with two facets. On the one hand, consciousness is equivalent to the "self" which feels, wills and judges. But this "self" or "I-ness" is not the entire area of consciousness. The other facet, also within consciousness but outside of "I-ness," contains the pictures, images and representations which comprise the world for us and which we experience. "This world lies outside of "I" (or *ego* or *self*) but not outside consciousness."[36]

The world, then, according to this rather novel formulation, does not lie outside the realm of consciousness. But, asks the contemporary Argentine philosopher, Vasallo, does it reside exclusively *within* consciousness? Korn does not answer the question. Nor does he imply that this is so. He merely rejects the claim that the world, as represented in consciousness, is a *copy* of what it *really* is. "The existence of this hypothetical world situated outside the realm which embraces our knowledge, has no *raison d'être*. Asserting its reality is only an act of faith . . ."[37] In short, human consciousness contains within itself two spheres: a "subjective" one (the realm of "I") and an "objective" one (the realm of the images and ideas which we experience as "world"). Thus, philosophy functions on two planes. In the objective realm, one starts with undeniable facts and then proceeds by means of proof to arrive inductively at controlled generalizations. The subjective area, on the other hand, involves human aspirations, beliefs, and all sorts of unmanageable and uncontrollable possibilities.

✶ ✶ ✶

Korn's idealist-inspired philosophic orientation examines the sources of error in the acquisition of knowledge. Like Bacon, he attacks prejudice in all of its manifestations: perception which is adversely conditioned by previously held conceptions; words which hide the nature of things; traditions which impose modes of thinking upon us.

It is essential that we free ourselves from all of the by-products of a "naive realism." Our consciousness lies at the basis of evaluation. Knowledge takes human consciousness as its point of departure, and this knowledge is gathered as a result of being faced with a problem, a problem which similarly exists in our consciousness. This universe of ours, in all of its tangible and visible manifestations, in fact, the very categories of space and time, can be known to us only as elements of our consciousness. It appears to us, therefore, as a mental phenomenon.[38] Nothing can be conceived of as being outside the realm of our consciousness. Even that which is assigned to the level of the sub-conscious is, by virtue of the mere fact that we can think of it, consigned to and thereby becomes part of the conscious. The moment we think of the unconscious, it ceases to be so.

Does this imply, then, that the universe, in spite of its apparent solidity, is nothing more than fiction? Not at all.

It is very real, regardless of whether we envisage the cosmos as a material or an ideal process. Reality can be viewed as movement, process and development—in terms of matter, energy or the psychic. "We prefer the latter, since this is the only way we have of knowing it. The rest is hypothesis."[39]

Nor does this mean that reality is a mental phenomenon. It simply means that this is the way in which it *presents* itself to us. It is theoretically possible for our thinking to reflect something different, i.e., for reality to be one thing and for our cognitive powers to be a reflection of something else. The essential difference between absolute idealism and extreme realism revolves precisely around this point: the identity of *modus cognoscendi* and *modus essendi*.

At one extreme, then, we have the position of absolute idealism which maintains that whatever is, exists only in consciousness. On the other hand, extreme realism views consciousness as a by-product of activities alien to ourselves. In the first case, as has already been pointed out, consciousness is the sole activity; in the second it is receptive and passive. Between these two extreme points of view there is room for various intermediate stages, i.e., eclectic approaches in the form of attempted compromises and syntheses.

There is no consciousness without content, just as there is no cognition without the act of knowing. In one's consciousness there merge facts, concepts and words:[40] facts by means of intuition which is basic, since it is spontaneous and immediate cognition constituted into a unity by perception; concepts, the result of elaborations of rational or logical ability; and finally, words as instruments of expression.[41]

Facts themselves cannot be defined; they are simply perceived in space and in time. To exist, then, means to be in space and time. The totality of all facts constitutes reality which embraces everything that exists in space and develops in time. Facts are born and die; far from being stable, they are characterized by continuous movement. They are also interrelated like links of a never-ending chain. In order to bring some order out of this apparent chaos, we make use of what is commonly referred to as a "concept."[42] A concept applies to an indefinite number of similar, successive or co-existent facts; it is the result of abstracting one or more common attributes from a group of facts, and is expressed in the form of a word or group of words.

This leads to polarization, characteristic of the process of concept formation, which involves the establishment and utilization of terms which designate contrary categories. These antinomies show the relationship of all elements of our experience. For example, the term "vertebrates" brings to mind its opposite, "invertebrates." This is a phenomenon which we ourselves have created and is a function of knowing, not of being. And so we have: "Spirit and Matter, Good and Evil, Freedom and Necessity, Absolute and Relative, Universal and Concrete, Being and Nothing, Subject and Object; Creator and Creation."[43]

In short, to think is to establish relationships, and the concept "relationships" itself, is meaningless outside the temporal-spatial reality. The concepts of space and time are pre-requisites for experiencing, as well as boundaries beyond which experience cannot go. And what are space and time? Are they aspects of external reality or are they forms which are inherent in the human mind? Are they modes of being or modes of knowing? Korn suggests that the second supposition seems more plausible: "space and time are mere forms of mental images."[44]

The distinction which Korn makes with respect to subject and object is reflected in his reference to culture. Object and subject are dependent upon each other. There is no subject without an object; there is no consciousness without content. In reciprocal fashion, from the standpoint of cognition, there is no object that can exist without a subject. The subject reacts in the presence of the object and his reaction is conditioned by the way in which the object satisfies or fails to satisfy his desires and purposes, his general view and orientation.

Culture, too, is the end result, the expression of the

human will. Its ingredients are accepted or rejected in accordance with human preferences. Natural sciences, in contrast to cultural studies, are structured according to the principle of causality; the latter, on the other hand, are guided by the principle of finality or purpose.

Experience is but fragmentary insofar as the totality of knowledge is concerned. There are always questions which go begging for answers, either because of the ignorance inherent within us, or the nature of the problems themselves. In fact, experience itself gives rise to the desire to go beyond it.

But man does not abandon the quest. Where experience fails him, where reason does not succeed in tying the loose ends together, man, in the face of new enigmas, resorts to that wonderful quality of his: imagination. He creates a supposed fact to be utilized in the search: an hypothesis.

"An hypothesis is an imagined fact, not given in experience."[45] However, an hypothesis is not a mere, irrational creation of the imagination. It must be grounded in reason, conditioned by material already known, and subject always to subsequent verification. This would serve to distinguish experience from science. "Science is objective experience, integrated by hypotheses."[46] Hence the need for constantly modifying and revising science; experience mounts and hypotheses are assumed and discarded.

In contrast to empirically-grounded hypotheses, we have hypostases which are creations of entities alien to temporal-spatial reality. An hypostasis is merely an affirmation of faith in the existence of a concept. This becomes a psychological necessity because of man's urgent wish to find solutions which are not readily available via experience or logic. This faith does not provide knowledge, but rather personal conviction and emotional comfort.

From this point, Korn passes on to a discussion of myths and mythology. A myth is a conception on the fringe of human experience, accepted on faith by a given group at a given period of time. Myths, ever since prehistoric times, have been an intrinsic part of the development of human culture. A myth can undergo modification; it can die and be replaced, but it will always be present. Every age, every social group, every culture has its constellation of myths. For myth is as primary a need as hunger: it interprets the secrets of the universe, as well as the enigma of one's own consciousness. The myth is the focal point of convergence for all the items that Korn has given us thus far: "the empirical datum which serves as the point of departure, the general or universal concept on which it rests, the hypothesis which justifies it, and the hypostasis which sanctions it."[47] For good or for bad, myth is the spiritual bond which gives group living its cohesiveness. Faith in the same myth binds men together: it may inspire sacrifice as well as self-interest. It is not the content of the myth which is historically important, but rather the number of its believers and the strength of their faith therein.

The fate of myths depends on the level of cultural advance. As new knowledge in the realm of experience is gained, myths evince a tendency to weaken. But not without resistance on their part. Myths may adopt new forms, attempt a more sophisticated garb, embed tenaciously in certain segments of the population after having been discarded by the more enlightened elements. For example, contemporary popular superstitions are but the residue of older beliefs. At times, myths of bygone days may even be perpetuated by interested groups.

A constellation of myths, systematized and bound together by a common thread, constitutes a mythology. Mythology is an attempt to explain phenomena caused by some agent other than man's will. At this point man becomes uneasy, if not fearful, and prone to submit to this alien agent. The religious myth is the result, a myth which "formulates the serious problem of the relationship between the concrete and the universal, between the individual and the totality, in search of a rational solution."[48]

The historical development of religious myths involves the creation and structuring of deities, as well as the institutionalization of objects, forms and houses of worship. The complexity of rites, liturgy and ceremonies gives rise to a specialized technique, to be exercised by a select group. Art, in its various forms, serves the great religious systems. The new priestly class begins to acquire power and in order to preserve it, has to engage in alliance with other social groups. Not only attacks from without but also inner divisions result in modifications.

New cosmic conceptions are born. Rebellion against authority and the exigencies of scientific investigation destroy old myths. Old systems of worship have lost their attraction for modern man. Does this mean that religious sentiment has been weakened, that man has lost his sense of connectedness with the eternal? No, for man will always be faced with the unknown and, hence, with a logical as well as emotional problem. Ritual, dogma and ceremony may disappear, but religious sentiment will always remain; in fact, the latter may persist without need of the former. If doubt will annihilate one myth, faith will immediately create another one to take its place.

How long can a dogmatic interpretation of the supernatural be considered valid? As long as it is supported by faith. Unfortunately faith dignifies even the absurd, The believer always finds reasons to defend his faith, asserts Korn, echoing Pascal, for "the heart has its own reasons which reason does not understand," Once, however, the concept of the supernatural is explained without resort to a pre-existent faith, then the religious position is abandoned. It is then that we enter the realm of metaphysics.[49]

Korn seemed convinced that it was impossible to leap, so to speak, from the *modus cognoscendi* to the *modus essendi*. Knowledge has its limits. But he was equally convinced that beyond the confines of empirical certitude lay a realm, closed to science, to be sure, yet accessible to the human spirit: the realm of the mystical and the artistic. "Art satisfies the metaphysical need by conciliating in esthetic emotion the opposition of the subjective and objective worlds."[50] It is an ideal truth, whether it be in the form of poetry, music or drama, which is reached via an esthetic vision, in the same way that the absolute is attained by metaphysical vision. The religious solution which inspires the conviction known as faith, has as its basis a genuine intensity of sentiment; it can become ecstatic and leads to mystical visions.

✓   ✓   ✓

The realm of the conscious is the theatre of operations which witnesses the agreements and disagreements between the subject which wills and judges, and the object which resists. The contacts between these two worlds, the "internal" and the "external," both residing within the realm of the conscious, give rise to mental forms which in turn regulate, coordinate, join and separate the various sensations experienced. This is done by means of concepts which are abstracted from both the subjective and objective areas.

Some concepts fall into disuse after having served their purpose and are replaced by others. On the other hand, there are concepts which resist being discarded. They would rather take over and, in fact, dominate consciousness, acquiring a life of their own, so to speak. The history of philosophy reveals instances of this sort: human consciousness and human thinking have been enslaved by the tyranny of these concepts, designated on occasion as innate ideas, *a priori* forms, categories. Undoubtedly these mental forms have played a useful role; they have served to systematize the data of our experience. Nevertheless, let us not put the cart before the horse. Following in the footsteps of Kant and Croce, Korn asserts that concepts are empty and meaningless without the intuitive content to which they apply. "To operate with concepts instead of intuitions is to invert hierarchies . . . conceptualism is the first step toward verbalism."[51] To intuit is the necessary prerequisite for knowing. By intuition is here meant "the spontaneous and immediate cognition constituted in unity by synthetic apperception."[52] Pure intuition does not exist, but the intuitive basis of knowledge must be recognized. The objective world, as we conceive it in our consciousness, has its characteristics and modalities, peculiar unto itself. It has measurable ex-

93

tension (temporal and spatial), quantity, and is subject to immutable laws; its processes are characterized by causal relationships. Its domain—devoid of purposiveness and morality—is made intelligible by the activities of science.

The objective sphere exists in space, which is itself an "element of human knowledge," rather than a reality which exists in and of itself, outside human consciousness. Space, time, quantity, cause and effect—these are all products of our consciousness. The laws of cause and effect are indicative of an order governed by an inflexible necessity, and therefore devoid of any possibility of freedom.

Fortunately, the objective world is not the whole of reality. As a matter of fact, reality "is a fossilized concept, i.e., a superstition."[53] Since the term itself stems from the Latin *res,* meaning "thing," it implies the idea of stability. Yet nothing is stable. Our consciousness observes dynamic processes and actions; in fact, "consciousness itself is not an entity, but action."[54] Philosophy should be written with verbs, rather than nouns, "actuality" as Aristotle taught us, rather than reality. An event then, is actualized within our consciousness, i.e., we make it relative to our consciousness; it does not exist as an absolute entity, separate and divorced therefrom.

Korn thus tries to avoid either extreme: the ego is not a product of the physical world, as realism would have us believe, nor is the world a creation of the ego—the end product of subjective idealism. The latter is akin to Rostand's rooster which believed that "if it did not crow, the sun would not rise."[55] Descartes' *cogito ergo sum* led to an identification of thinking with the ego. This led to the German idealistic systems which confused consciousness with *my* consciousness, and which substituted the part for the whole.

The realists opposed this fallacious conception. They demonstrated the independence of subject and object. But, according to Korn, they detracted from their achievement by endeavoring to bring the subject under the control of a noumenal world. "The objective world is certainly outside of the ego, but not outside of consciousness."[56]

Once again the point is made: the objective world obeys necessary laws. Events can be foreseen; causes produce effects. No finality is involved. On the other hand, the subjective world is free, i.e., in the sense that action is *willed,* purposes are *projected* into the future. The subject "is shaken by sorrow or joys, it affirms or denies, it forms purposes, forges ideals . . . and subordinates its conduct to the ends it pursues."[57]

Its freedom, however, is one of desiring, not doing, since it is continually circumscribed by the coercion of necessity. The subject is therefore in an act of constant rebellion, endeavoring to make its power equal to its wish. It utilizes science and technology to overcome the resistance and subdue nature. Yet it does not seek to annihilate the resistance it encounters in the objective world, but rather to reduce it in order to attain its goal. Indeed, it is akin to Kant's dove which would come hurtling down "if it did not support itself on the resistance which opposes it."[58]

But not only is the subject limited by the realm of the objective: it is also disturbed by its own emotions, impulses and errors. To mastery of nature is therefore added mastery of self. Economic liberty is supplemented by ethical liberty; both comprise the totality of human freedom. One cannot exist without the other; both constitute the basis for the development of human personality.

We are constrained to bear with the dictates of natural, physical law. By contrast we shape and dictate the moral law. The former is an expression of the kingdom of necessity; the latter, a product of our free will. We must perforce obey the one; we may disobey the other. And Korn puts it succinctly as well as dramatically: "From the depths of consciousness, the self emerges like a torso: its forehead free, its arms free, resolved to liberate the remainder."[59] The remainder, by implication, is the creation of culture, for which human freedom is the necessary prerequisite. Culture implies the creation of value.

In the realm of the subjective, Korn's approach would lead directly toward a philosophy of personality. The subject, although he cannot operate without his antagonist, the object, nevertheless strives to unfold and develop in the face of obstacles constantly put in his path by the object. He exercises his free will, he feels himself to be master of his actions, he is an autonomous being; he experiences joy and sorrow, he affirms or denies, and formulates ideals, ends and purposes which he considers to be of value. His ultimate goal is the fullest development of his personality. By means of freedom, dignity and responsibility, he seeks to subordinate the natural order to the moral order. Freedom cannot operate in a vacuum; the forces of necessity must be recognized. In the constant stress and strain between the two, human will is stimulated and exercised, although freedom itself is never fully attained. Freedom, as an end in itself, comments Pucciarelli in his essay on Korn, "consists of liberation from all coercion in the economic and ethical realms."[60]

Freedom, then, as the distinguishing characteristic of human action, is not only a means, but an end in itself. It is the motive force which guides our actions as we seek to dominate all coercive elements, whether from within or without, whether in the sphere of the material or the realm of the moral. In the process, man achieves an ever-increasing measure of freedom.

Man strives to attain a position of mastery, not one of servitude. He is the ultimate measure of all values. He is not only an animal. Human culture is the very trait that introduces distance between man and animal, and makes life something more than the satisfaction of bodily appetites. Life would be absurd if it were not dignified with some higher purpose. For this reason, man is a value-creating being. In order to create values, he needs freedom.

Man is continually acting, reacting, constructing, modifying. Each generation carries the process forward in unending fashion: it therefore builds and amends systems of values. History is nothing more than a never-ending evolution of human value systems.

It is an illusion to speak in terms of universal values, i.e., values which are invariable and applicable to all men at all times. Objects do not possess value if no one appreciates them or if they do not affect human interests. Rather than speak of universal values, it would be more accurate to place the emphasis on the universality of the evaluating consciousness.

So-called absolute, permanent and unchangeable values, or values "in themselves," are for Korn an abstract denomination of final, as yet unrealized aspirations. One cannot say that they *are;* they *become.* We can *think* about this ideal structure, but we do not experience it.

Korn, then, does not admit that values are ideal entities that impose themselves on man's consciousness. This would amount to coercion.

Coercion and freedom are antinomies found in the area of subjective data (as distinguished from objective). Coercion is basic; freedom is simply absence of coercion. Both play their part in the course of human existence. The extent of freedom achieved by man is a measure of his personal dignity. But in order to achieve freedom, one must be conscious of coercion. Coercion exists in three areas: in nature, in social groupings, and within oneself. Hence, man strives to achieve freedom by fighting against the forces of nature, by resisting and controlling group pressures of society, and by vanquishing the internal pressures within himself. In this way, he attains control over the forces of nature, effects an adequate social organization, and shapes himself into a self-directing organism. In each instance, an act of will is involved; his will power thus leads him to an act of evaluation.

Values, then, have their matrix in the autonomy of the human personality. Korn's entire ethical structure is predicated upon this premise. Human action is the exercise of the will, and the will is free and responsible. In fact, responsible action is not only a correlative but a result of free will; freedom and responsibility make ethics possible. Unlike the

97

Positivists who looked upon free will as a "subjective illusion," Korn attacked determinism as being incompatible with the very establishment of morality. In his essay entitled, "Incipit Vita Nova," he declares: "An ethical system is impossible without obligations, without responsibility, without sanctions, and especially without liberty. The new philosophy will free us from the nightmare of mechanical automatism, and will give back to us the dignity of our free and conscious personality, mistress of its destiny."[61]

Freedom, however, is not absolute. One must strive continually to increase its scope against the forces of coercion and necessity. Moreover, the entire problem of freedom has become complicated because, under the influence of Positivism, the phenomena of the physical world have been equated with those of the psychic realm. Korn disagrees. Physical phenomena are necessary or contingent, but never free. Only human acts can be free, and if they are not, it is because they are subject to coercion.[62]

Freedom and ethics are related to the problem of action, i.e., actualized will. By means of action, man breaks out of his isolation and establishes the subject-object relationship. It is through action that man has created culture. And it is through culture that man pursues and achieves his freedom from all slavery. "Culture is the work of the will: the will desires freedom."[63]

Economic freedom which implies mastery of the objective world, and ethical freedom which points towards mastery of oneself, presuppose each other, i.e., one cannot exist without the other; both are basic. Nor should they be confused. "The useful is not always good, nor is the good always useful."[64]

To mistake the useful for the good is to commit the error of all utilitarian morality. Yet the lack of economic freedom would tend to make us exchange ethical freedom for a bowl of lentils; conversely, the absence of ethical liberty leaves the way open for the complete domination of man by instincts and dogmas.

The determinism of the objective realm cannot be denied; nor can one shut one's eyes to the world of utilitarian egoism. By the same token, one cannot and should not deny individual freedom and responsibility or suppress the dignity of human personality which continually seeks ever widening and deepening areas for development. We make use of objective determinism only to achieve material freedom. "But to limit ourselves to this end is to convert ourselves into slaves of the machine we have invented."[65]

Morality without sanctions is ridiculous. Such a state would imply action devoid of purpose. Our acts, judged pragmatically, are efficient or harmful, the result of ignorance or knowledge. An ethical act cannot be subjected to utilitarian sanctions, because in that case it could no longer be considered ethical. In analogous fashion, an esthetic pleasure is not to be thought of as useful. If ethical finality is one of achieving freedom, then sanctions applied to an immoral act are calculated to result in a loss of freedom, "the degradation of human freedom." Conversely, a good act "has its compensation in itself, i.e., in the consciouness of actualized freedom."[66] Man has always struggled to increase the range of his freedom, more so since he emerged from his state of animality. The struggle will reach its culminating point and will end, only when freedom and necessity will have become reconciled.

Creative freedom, then, is not merely an attempt to free man from his dependence upon the economic factor of the physical mechanism imbedded in the environment. It is not an attempt to rid us of our impulses which prolong within us this state of dependence upon the material. Nor is it equivalent to fanciful creation or invention of capriciously subjective values. It aspires, rather, toward and yearns to be itself for the sake of itself, and can achieve complete autonomy only within the fullest development of the human personality. All other evaluations emerge from this single source and tend to attain this common goal, namely, the affirmation of the autonomy of the personality.

From this basic drive there has emerged, as a result, the collective effort of the human species, known as culture— the product of the affirmation of freedom as opposed to the kingdom of necessity. "Because freedom is not given to us, it is necessary to win it for ourselves within the brief span of our individual lives, as well as in the course of the progressive evolution of collective living. This end desire is fertile; therefore we have called it Creative Liberty."[67] Personality is thus the last word.

At this point a distinction must be made between two terms: evaluation and value. Evaluation implies reaction on the part of the subject with respect to an object. This is a rather complex configuration and process, involving such factors as biological needs, hereditary inclinations, habits, prejudices, impulses, interests and associations. The final decision with reference to the object. i.e., the evaluating process, is determined by the personality of the individual which is conditioned by all of the above-mentioned conditioning factors, all uniting in an over-all synthesis. An object, then, is said to have value, after this evaluating process has reached its culmination. Evaluation is the reaction to a fact on the part of the human will. What is involved is summed up in the phrase: "I want it" or "I don't want it." "Value is the object of affirmative evaluation."[68]

One must distinguish between two processes: the natural and the historical. Man develops his activity *vis-à-vis* nature, i.e., in the process of dealing with his environment he endeavors to fathom it, to know it, not only because of his intellectual curiosity, but because it affects him emotionally. As a result, he judges, appreciates, evaluates: he *creates* value. This is what essentially distinguishes the natural process from the historical process. The former does no more than establish a cause-and-effect relationship. On the other hand, the historical process is one in which man involves himself, forming opinions and judgments concerning these causal relationships. This is the heart of value theory.[69]

Values have to be arranged in some kind of hierarchical order or system and their validity established.[70] This is the task of a philosophy of values. In setting up a table of values, it is soon realized that for every given ideal value, there is a corresponding historical or relative value. For example, the ideal of justice is expressed historically by the law, which is far from absolute. Legal concepts are born, modified, and may eventually disappear. They are, there-fore, an expression of historical reality, whereas justice is an ideal concept and therefore absolute.

Korn proposes a scheme involving three groups of value systems:

1. Biological evaluations: these include economic, in-stinctive and erotic factors;
2. Social and vital evaluations;
3. Cultural evaluations, which refer to and are in-herent in religious, ethical, logical and esthetic ac-tivities.[71]

Each evaluation corresponds to a polarization involving two basic concepts (one positive, the other, negative), as well as a value which is historically capable of being realized and one which must perforce remain in the realm of the ideal. For example, in the field of logic, the basic concepts involved are true and false. Knowledge is that which is cap-able of realization; truth is the ideal which recedes con-tinually into the future.

Since an individual acts in a multiplicity of environ-ments, e.g., economic, political, social and religious, each with its circumstantial complexes peculiar unto itself, he has to distinguish and classify: useful and harmful, pleasant and repugnant, right and wrong, etc. Various factors and motivations, overt as well as subtle, determine his reactions. Ideal concepts condition his reaction to concrete manifesta-tions. It is in this connection that Korn presents us with the following table of values:[72]

Evaluations	Basic concepts	Ideal ends	Historical values	Example of philosophical system
1. Economic	Useful—harmful	Well-being	Technology	Utilitarianism
2. Instinctive	Agreeable—disagreeable	Happiness	Pleasure	Hedonism
3. Erotic	Lovable—hateful	Love	Family	Mysticism
4. Vital	Select—common	Power	Discipline	Pragmatism
5. Social	Lawful—prohibited	Justice	Law	Sociological systems
6. Religious	Holy—profane	Holiness	Worship	Scholasticism
7. Ethical	Good—evil	Good	Morality	Stoicism
8. Logical	True—false	Truth	Knowledge	Rationalism
9. Esthetic	Beautiful—ugly	Beauty	Art	Intuitionism

Do absolute values exist? Korn asks again, values which are constant and universal? They exist only insofar as we think of them as such, only insofar as we strive to attain them but never quite succeed. They are abstract, unreal concepts, products of an idealistic framework, criteria to be utilized in the structuring of our real world of data.[73]

Values have their origin in experience, in pragmatic necessity; they vary according to the needs and reactions to the environment on the part of the particular social group, and are therefore subject to continual change.

Since values originate in the process of man's interaction with his environment, it follows that they cannot be immutable or eternal. Values are relative because they always exist in relation to their cultural setting. "To imagine that values, created in the struggle for freedom, are durable and objective, is to be unaware of their transitory nature."[74] The ideal expression of a given value, i.e., its highly idealized state, can be realized only partially.

If, therefore, values are subjective, they cannot exist independently, i.e., they are contingent upon the process of evaluation itself. Logically, this in itself would preclude the structuring of any hierarchy of values, since the very act of attempting to establish such a hierarchy is a subjective evaluation.

In view of the apparently subjective nature of value, one is tempted to assume that such relativism can lead only to complete nihilism. But, actually, in practice, things do not happen quite this way. Although evaluation is an individual act, the individual himself does not live in isolated fashion; he is not a law unto himself. Human interests and aspirations are shared in common, and these result in values which are likewise common, shared in by at least a majority of the group. Similarly, the acceptance of a hierarchy of values is a group affair, the consensus of judgments at a given historical moment, determined by specific circumstances.[75]

The problem of values is, in the last analysis, equivalent to the problem of culture, the problem of man's sense of life. For it is values which give meaning to man's life. These, according to Korn, constitute the proper domain of philosophy; philosophy is nothing more than axiology.

On the other hand, science deals with the realm of objective fact. "For science there are no values, there are simply facts, equally interesting or equally indifferent. When we attribute value to a thing, we are doing something involving risk; it is not the same for me as for another, it is not the same today as yesterday. The circumstantial value of real objects depends on our evaluation."[76]

There are no values independent of evaluation. Evaluation is a psychological process. Rather than being a logical operation, it is an attitude. The person who evaluates may do so rationally, but in doing so, he utilizes reason to further his purposes. Where, then are we to find the matrix, common to all evaluation? And Korn answers: In the human personality.[77]

"All evaluations emerge from only one source and tend toward the same end. They affirm the autonomy of the Personality, they pursue its emancipation from all servitude, that is, its liberation as the ultimate and common purpose. Relative liberty in each case, absolute liberty as the ideal goal. From this impulse have been born the fruits of culture, the historical striving of the species, the affirmation of liberty vis-à-vis the domination of necessity."[78]

In short, man fixes values; man also denies them. His will is sovereign. Evaluation resides in man's sovereign will, in his personality. And man's personality "is found in a world which it wants to and should reform because that world is evil."[79]

Values, then, are the end product resulting from the activity of the will, and the will, in turn, is often motivated by impulse, emotion, bias. But is this always so? Not necessarily. Value judgments are not always *completely* subject to a person's preferences. One critic has stated that Korn did not bother to analyze properly "the difference between

103

the act of evaluating an object and the properties or reasons which make it worthy of being evaluated . . ."[80]

Korn himself reveals the tragic hiatus which has made man unhappy, namely, the gap that exists between his desperate attempts to embrace a secure, all-inclusive absolute, and his melancholy acceptance of a fleeting, unstable relativism. For example: "In consciousness, the absolute is presented as aspiration, as the tendency toward a purpose that we value as supreme and ultimate, as the overcoming of subject-object duality . . . To actualize absolute liberty by the attainment of economic mastery over nature and of ethical self-control, to submit necessity to liberty, to reach the full development of one's own personality: there is the goal . . ."[81]

Compare the above quotation with the following: ". . . we know nothing but the unextended instant between the past and the future: a perpetual and fugitive present. We know nothing but the incessant passage of particular and relative events. Neither the eternal nor the absolute is in our intuition."[82]

If only we could be certain of knowing the absolute, then we would be at peace. We feel keenly the relativity that afflicts us. Man strives to arrive at the absolute and makes use of metaphysics, art and religion to satisfy the hunger of his spirit. "Metaphysics offers systems which are not the expression of what is verified, but hypothetical constructions of creative imagination."[83] They are not constructed by means of reasoning. They are rather, the product, in the form of psychological awareness, of an attempt by the will to deal with an obsessive problem. Sometimes this product may be the final stage of a long, drawn-out incubation period; at other times, it may be caused by a spontaneous inspiration or intuition. Rational argumentation which seeks to explain it appears upon the scene subsequently.

Would it be too much to assume that man remains dissatisfied with a relativistic frame of reference, although he must perforce make his peace therewith and accept it as a reality in his day-to-day existence? Does he not continually strive to grasp the ever-elusive absolute? And do not his dissatisfaction and disquietude justify his constant search, a search for something that cannot be demonstrated empirically?

Is not this search the result of man's desire to know the *noumenon?* Is not his yearning to transcend the duality of subject-object the very stuff and substance of metaphysics? And aren't metaphysical solutions, whatever they may be, nothing more than hypotheses created by human imagination, the result of psychological needs, which are subsequently rationalized?

As has already been pointed out, Korn advances the interesting observation that metaphysics resembles religion. In either case, reason attempts to interpret the unknown or the supernatural. However, the metaphysician utilizes rational arguments, not because of a general feeling of fear and insecurity, which is perhaps the case in religion, but rather out of intellectual curiosity vis-à-vis the enigma of existence.[84]

Nevertheless, since metaphysics implies knowledge devoid of empirical content, it is referred to as "metaphysical myth" in contrast to "religious myth." Yet even so, it cannot be dismissed lightly. The need for metaphysics cannot be extinguished, even though we shall never find a solution. And this is tragic. Behold the paradox: "metaphysics is necessary, metaphysics is impossible."[85] It is an aspiration which will never be satisfied. It has given rise to great philosophic systems: realism, absolute idealism and subjective idealism. The various contemporary schools of philosophic thought are merely variations of ancient themes. Such movements as neo-Scholasticism, neo-Realism, neo-Idealism, neo-Romanticism, neo-Hegelianism or neo-Positivism, are but evidence that it is impossible to turn one's back on the "metaphysical myth." Although the metaphysical problem exists, metaphysical knowledge does not. But all is not in vain. The "myth" has its value. It reveals "contradictory aspects of reality . . . it makes us conscious of our power and our impotence." We seek the absolute and find instead our "I," i.e., metaphysics "replaces simple ignorance by conscious ignorance."[86] Once we abandon the possibility of absolute knowledge, we concentrate our attention upon ourselves and our world, and upon the possibility of a relative conception of our spatio-temporal reality. In short, metaphysics is reduced to pure yearning; it operates symbolically without any hope of ever reaching its goal. For, in essence, it seeks the reconciliation of opposites. But these endure; the conflict continues since we cannot transcend and operate beyond our own consciousness which, as we have seen, produces these antinomies.

✓ ✓ ✓

Philosophic currents, prevalent in Korn's lifetime, stressed the principle of dynamic change, taking the evolutionary doctrines as their point of departure. Even natural laws were no longer conceived of as immutable. The unknowable, so dear to the hearts of the Positivists as an area to avoid, had now been met head-on. The immanence in reality of an active principle—whether this be called energy, élan vital, will or spirit—was a concept incorporated into the general configuration of the newer currents of philosophic thought.

Korn refers to the attempt by the metaphysics of his day to bridge the gap between the natural sciences on the one hand, and those of the spirit, or the cultural sciences as he refers to them, on the other. How can cosmic and human activity be brought together into one great synthesis?

Metaphysics had tried to reduce dualities to a unitary principle. Positivism had aspired to do the same, i.e., to offer a monistic explanation of all problems in terms of scientific law. But the contradictions persisted nevertheless. For centuries man believed in the existence of two distinct substances: body and soul, matter and spirit, etc. Some philosophies, at various intervals, tried to eliminate one or the other of the two terms of the antinomy, e.g., they stated that psychic activity depended on organic physical or psychological phenomena, or else, that matter was nothing more than an activity created by the spirit.

Pre-Kantian philosophy had considered existing reality

as a fixed and definite entity. One had but to ascertain the immutable standards which governed this entity and all subsequent problems would be resolved. In contrast, philosophy which followed Kant abandoned this static approach and adopted instead the dynamic principle which maintained that reality is always in motion and subject to perpetual change. The evolutionary principle which is basic to the post-Kantian orientation was the object of 19th century philosophic investigation. In this connection, Korn refers briefly to several attempts to discover the operation of this principle, namely, those made by Bergson, Dilthey and Marx.

There are two ways of resolving the conflict involved in a dualism.[87] Either the two contrasting components are synthesized into a higher concept, or else, one of the components is merely truncated. Bergson attributed to the physical world an existence which is only apparent; what really exists is the spiritual world, the reality of the vital impulse which is always creating new forms.[88] By comparing the physical world to a movie film that passes through our consciousness, Bergson placed himself squarely in the camp of the idealists for whom the external world is but a mental image. However, Korn views with sympathy Bergson's attempt to rise above the Positivist's approach to the possibility of metaphysical cognition. Intuition is a means toward making greater strides along the road to the absolute.

For Dilthey, Korn comments briefly, the problem of evolution is mental, i.e., it takes place in man's psychic activity.[89] Philosophic systems are simply historical episodes which have developed at a given moment in the course of cultural evolution. The very concept, e.g., that we have of science at the moment is part and parcel of this historical evolutionary process.

Korn's interest in Marxism is the result of his political sensitivities which can be linked to his interest in human freedom. Freedom in this instance means emancipation from all obstacles which impede human development. Freedom is both economic and moral. Here Korn agrees with

Marx: the economic is a prerequisite for the moral. Korn protests against the so-called vulgarizers of Marx, i.e., those who claim that Marx spoke only of the economic factor. Marx never denied the existence of a psychic, cultural world which he labelled "super-structure" and which rested, as it were, on the economic base.[90] However, Korn maintains that this superstructure is, at times, quite important, as much so, perhaps, as the basic economic structure.

The ethical factor is decisive in the evolution of human existence. The moral character of a person may conceivably exert an influence upon the solution of practical problems. Marx may have exaggerated the importance of the economic factor and have offered us an excessively unilateral theory; it is conceivable that at times certain elements in the so-called superstructure may exert an unexpectedly powerful influence upon the march of events, perhaps even upon the basic structure itself. One must guard against oversimplification and be careful to distinguish between unilateral economic *causation* and economic *determinism*.

The basis of Positivism, Korn reminds us, was scientific systematization. When this systematization broke down, due to the advances made by science itself, a crisis set in and the reaction was not long in making its appearance. This took the form of a resurgent interest in speculation which attempted to go beyond the confines of empirical knowledge. Reality was again split in two: the realm of the natural or physical sciences, and that which Korn chooses to call the world of cultural sciences in which human personality was reaffirmed. Korn examines the various attempts on the part of this metaphysical resurgence to formulate satisfactory meta-empirical solutions. Many are the representatives of this upsurge. Croce, e.g., based himself chiefly on Hegel, and affirmed that all that exists is simply an expression of the development of the universal idea. For Croce, the humanist, the upsurge of science in the 19th century is not of primary importance; scientific progress is an unknown and even alien factor. Hence, science does not really capture reality; empiricism cannot penetrate the essence of things. Croce thus amputates one of the terms of the antinomy, an operation which leaves Korn far from satisfied.[91]

In his study of some of the writings of the great figures in philosophical thought, Korn concurs with some and disagrees with others. Furthermore, in the case of some philosophers, he is careful to select only certain portions of their contributions, rejecting others. For example, he agrees with Kant in the belief that it is a human characteristic to experience the need for a metaphysics, a need in which reason, emotion and will each play a part.[91a] Korn also believes, together with Kant, that the absolute is unattainable, not only by way of the senses, but via rational knowledge. Human cognition encounters obstacles which it cannot overcome. However, he disagrees with Kant concerning the question of freedom. Kant had placed freedom in the realm of the noumena. Korn, by contrast, asserts that freedom is a very real entity embedded in one's consciousness. How, asks Korn, can the fact that freedom is consigned to the sphere of the noumena, be reconciled with a determinism which characterizes the phenomenal world?[92] Noumenal freedom cannot be adjusted to phenomenal determinism. Freedom is either a vibrant fact within one's consciousness or else it does not exist. Korn affirms its existence by advancing his favorite formula: "the dualism of subject and object is reduced, precisely, to the opposition between freedom and necessity."[93] Freedom and necessity co-exist. Can one be responsible for his actions without being free? What is necessary is objective, i.e., the entire chain of facts and events linked to the principle of causality which lies beyond the realm of individual free-will. In its presence the subject has but to act and react according to his values and purposes. These, in turn, are an expression of his will; if everything were to obey the law of necessity, the subject would disappear. Moreover, Kant is in error by virtue of having ignored the dynamic nature of the universe; one must recognize the evolving principle as a necessary category in order to know reality.

Korn also discusses the thinking of the neo-Kantians, who had tried to restore and go beyond the philosophical tradition of Kant, a tradition which had been interrupted by the upsurge of science and positivism. The neo-Kantians concerned themselves with those problems which science and positivism could not deal with satisfactorily, in short, with such problems as culture, history and values. In this discussion, too, as on previous occasions, Korn rejects the objectivist interpretation of the term "universe" which holds that both the world and the subject ("I") are contained within the concept "universe." This approach takes the object as its point of departure and imprisons the subject, so to speak, within its fold. Such an approach jeopardizes individuality, freedom and personal responsibility.

Korn's interpretation of the term "universe," places the objective world and the subjective "I" in opposition to each other. Objects are not real in themselves; they depend, rather, on the subject. It is through the subject's reactions and activities that the essence of the objects can be ascertained. This, of course, is the purely subjective position which reduces the objective world to mere appearance and, instead, raises man's activity and freedom to a level of supreme importance.

However, it should be borne in mind that Korn avoids extreme subjectivism, i.e., the position which would reduce the object to a mere projection of the subject's activity. Instead, object and subject are but two fragments of reality which face each other, as it were, in knowledge and in action.

Knowledge of objective reality belongs to the preserves of science. It is philosophy's task to explore the realm of values. Nor are values to be restricted to the private terrain of the subject. Philosophy also has to explore the cultural and historical world in order to carry out its task effectively.

Whether he is dealing with Pascal or St. Augustine or Kant, Korn will always return to the central theme: the importance of the human personality. Pascal, e.g., is important because he represents an attitude which emphasizes ethical values. Pascal's importance lies in "the accentuation of human personality, as a problem superior to cosmic problems."[94]

✓ ✓ ✓

Professor Kilgore, in his penetrating study, has suggested that Korn failed to clear up a serious problem within the realm of value theory, namely: Is an object of evaluation, speaking empirically, worthy of evaluation in a normative sense?[95] Furthermore, does Korn seem to identify, e.g., what is good with what is desired instead of with that which deserves to be evaluated when he states that evaluation is simply "a psychological process," "an attitude?"[96]

Korn's conception of philosophy as value theory would leave one with the uncomfortable feeling that either values embrace a far more extensive area than is commonly supposed, or else, as Kilgore asserts, a segment of material which "traditionally belongs in the realm of philosophy is excluded for arbitrary and unjustifiable reasons."[97] In this respect, Korn may conceivably have been as guilty as the Positivists he criticized: both restricted the area of philosophic inquiry.

It should also be pointed out that freedom is not only absence of coercion, i.e., affording the possibility of choosing between two or more alternatives. Obviously, if there is only one alternative, there can be no freedom of action. Freedom is also a matter of degree: whatever alternatives exist may be amplified and new possibilities envisaged. This would place the whole concept of freedom within a more dynamic framework. Furthermore, one should distinguish between a person who knows that he has freedom of action, and one who doesn't but thinks he has. Even in the case of the person who exercises freedom of choice, one may profitably ask to what extent the alternative selected is really free, i.e., whether its selection has not been determined by other factors.[98]

One fact remains certain, and this is an outstanding characteristic of Korn's axiology: His was a philosophy of movement, of dynamism. It was this orientation which placed him squarely in opposition to Plato's fixed and immovable forms. Creative freedom *needs* coercion in order to thrive. In this respect, creative freedom for the individual is a response to a stimulus provided by society. Yet the dilemma which results from the postulation of the problem in this form is obvious: at which point can society's stimulus, i.e., coercion in the name of maintaining "order," become so strong that individual liberty is snuffed out? Conversely, given the dynamic relationship between the two, at which point in this relationship do "order" and "stability" cease to function effectively because of the demands made in the name of fostering creative liberty for the individual? We cannot be too harsh with Korn for his failing to have clarified the issue satisfactorily. Philosophers have wrestled with this problem in the past, and others will undoubtedly continue to do so.

CHAPTER FOUR

Francisco Romero

ALTHOUGH THE ORACLE of Delphi proclaimed the need for man to know himself, it isn't until the 19th century, and perhaps more acutely so in our own, that man as a problem begins to be the subject of study. Philosophical essays on the nature of man and his place in the universe reveal a never-ending concern and perplexity.

The causes for this anthropological interest are not difficult to find. The obvious ones can be said to be: 1. The world crisis which man has been experiencing, especially in the present century; 2. The more subtle conflicts resulting from contrasting philosophical approaches which attempt to explain man from the traditionally religious point of view, within the framework of idealistic system, or in scientific and naturalistic terms.

If one really preferred to trace one's steps historically, then perhaps it could be said that the Renaissance produced the first crisis.[1] It was then that the heliocentric theory rudely awakened man to the fact that he was no longer the center of the universe. Successive hammer blows to his ego produced additional crises. Linnaeus and Darwin, science and materialism—and all the consequences that followed— left their imprint. Man was no longer a divine creation; man was a rational animal; man was a mere animal; man was a machine; man was a cog in a machine. Man, in short, no longer knew what he was. As Max Scheler puts it, "He knows that he doesn't know."[2]

Influenced by Scheler as well as by Dilthey, Husserl, N.

Hartmann, and the older giants of German philosophic thought, Francisco Romero devoted the best of his energies to the field of philosophical anthropology.

Romero's principal interest concerned the nature and function of the person, a theme to which he dedicated himself for some time beginning with an article entitled *Filosofía de la persona,* (1944)[3] and developed subsequently in more extensive and comprehensive fashion in *Teoría del hombre,*[4] which appeared eight years later.

Romero posits the basic problem in terms of man's duality,[5] i.e., individual versus person, face versus mask, psyche versus spirit, egoism versus altruism, subjective utilitarianism versus objective universalism.

Man oscillates in his behavior pattern, says Romero, between two opposing poles of conduct. On the one hand, he follows a subjective pattern and obeys purely utilitarian motives and egotistic impulses. On the other hand, he seeks objective orientation: he aspires toward values and modes of conduct which go beyond personal convenience and narrow interests, and which are less utilitarian and less self-centered. In other words, this dual nature of man poses the problem of satisfaction of natural appetites versus occasions or instances wherein man asserts truth or justice unconditionally, i.e., regardless of individual preference. Philosophically, this reduces itself to the conflict between the naturalistic, pseudo-empirical tendency which denies man's autonomy, and the opposing school of thought which affirms and postulates the existence of objectivity and universality within man.

In the first case, i.e., where self-centered intentionality prevails, we have a picture of what Romero designates as the *individual.* It is here that the *psyche* dominates; subjective motivations prove stronger. In the second instance, man's intentionality transcends the merely subjective; it goes beyond individual interests. In fact, it is a "disinterested" interest, in the sense that human energy is expended for the sake of the value itself, or to the degree that *what is* measures up to *what ought to be.* In this latter instance,

Romero refers to the human being as a *person;* the guiding principle here is the *spirit* which projects human intentionality toward universality and objectivity. At the risk of oversimplification, one can perhaps formulate the principle involved as a mathematical ratio: psyche is to individual as spirit is to person.

At times the person or spirit appears to be asleep, in which case the individual psyche has free rein. At others, it tells the psyche what ought to be done, but without being able to compel it to do so. On occasion, it may even impose its law upon the psyche. In any case, individual and person are in constant conflict.

Particularly interesting is Romero's reference to "face" and "mask," as being analogous to "individual" and "person," respectively.[6] Here Romero combines philology with philosophy.* Referring to Klages' and Vossler's interpretations of the word *persona,* he reminds us that the mask was always used to hide the actor's individuality, or rather, to give another personality to the actor. The term "person" derives from the Latin *personare,* which means "to echo or resound by way of." The comparison is striking. When we act as a "person," we tend to de-individualize ourselves, to get away from ourselves. Of course, Romero is quick to point out that even this very attractive comparison has its weaknesses. The face is vital, whereas the mask is rigid. By extension, the individual is natural and alive; the person is artificial, remotely ideal, fictitious.[6a]

Yet the comparison is essentially a sound one. The individual *strives* to become a person, just as the actor aspires to transcend himself and become the character personified by the mask. The "person" is just as remote as a mask or an ideal; both have to be realized by aspiring, as has already been suggested, to the state of future "ought-ness," rather than the "is-ness" of the present.

Of the two, psyche and spirit, the first is stronger,

* The Latin *persona* refers to the character portrayed by the actor. The meaning of the Greek term, of which the Latin is a derivative, is more concrete. It refers to the mask which covers the face of the actor.

tougher, predominant. The second, the spirit, is weaker; it is a more recent arrival upon the scene of reality, and therefore has not yet had a chance to grow tough. It is easy to do away with a newborn creature, but it doesn't therefore follow, that the recent arrival doesn't or didn't exist.

In comparison with the other forms of reality, e.g., material or physical reality, life and psyche, the spirit may be said to have been born just yesterday. Spirit is conceivably concomitant with the beginning of history. The others date from the dark, unknown abyss of time.

The spirit depends and feeds on the psyche, but cannot be reduced to psyche, just as the psyche, in turn, depends on life itself but is not identified with life; or just as life itself is nourished by inert mass or substance, but is never confused with that substance.

The animal (and man, insofar as he is animal) views his immediate reality, his environment, as merely an extension of his own vital sphere, as an occasion where things happen which are or are not useful to him. His immediate reality thus takes on a purely subjective character.

Man, on the other hand, as a spiritual being, views his reality somewhat differently. He objectifies it, i.e., he endows it with meaning and configuration which are independent of him. He may or may not be the recipient of its influences. He is not content with knowing the significance which things existing in this reality (in the world or universe or cosmos) have for him. He tries, rather, to find out what these things are like "in themselves," so to speak, independent of him.

And so, in orienting himself toward a world of objective things, things which are not appearances but essences, he also, in the process, struggles to find his way to other forms of objectivity, toward the area of values, values which exist objectively, without reference to subjective appetites, desires or whims which are transitory and have to be satisfied.

"The *person* is the *spiritual* individual,"[7] the totality, the complex of spiritual acts and attitudes in each individual. The person is rigidly uniform, objective, and is structured over the individual's psyche. The function of the person is to command the individual. But this does not mean that the person always succeeds in commanding under all circumstances, at every moment. Let us remember what we said about the relatively recent origin of this "infant;" that is why it is still somewhat weak.

Individual and person are thus always in conflict. First one triumphs, then the other, depending upon the circumstances. The individual is dominated by habit, custom, subjective interests. The person is a behavior pattern determined by principles, by pure values. Man becomes a person to the degree that he can transcend his empirical appetites and needs, and arrive at the super-individual realm, namely, the objective, constantly rigid condition of the person, as opposed to the changeable fleeting, ephemeral condition of the individual.

The individual evaluates everything in terms of what it can do for him. The person evaluates everything in terms of what it is worth in and of itself. The existence and affirmation of values are essential to the person. The history of the spirit has its heroes, those who have affirmed the values found in their space-time milieu, or who have discovered new values. The persons have always been the guides, the teachers. Individuals have always needed to be shown. Many have been so blind that they didn't even want to be shown.

Moreover, the person needs to live in the community, among people, not in splendid isolation, in order to receive from them the necessary stimulus and sustenance, in order to guide and goad. Spirit must reside within culture, not outside of it. There is a reciprocal relationship between the two. Spirit creates culture and is in turn nurtured thereby. Ethical values, then, are values of the person, and are found only within the person. The person disintegrates if he is removed from his group; he is strengthened to the extent that he mingles with people.

If only the individual, rather than the person, prevails within man, we have a condition described by Hobbes, where only that which *is*—is right.[8] Only that which man can

117

exploit should exist—and things exist precisely to be exploited. This is a state where jungle law prevails. Individuals are in perpetual, continuous conflict. Man is a wolf devouring other wolves. Any restraints which are imposed are done so for the convenience of the wolves themselves, and these are usually imposed by a powerful agent.

Realistically, Hobbes' position seems justified. Man is more frequently an individual than a person. But the spirit also exists, and must be reckoned with. Every society is both a society of individuals and a society of persons. There is always a conflict between material interests and ideal interests. And every society should see to it that the number of individuals decrease and the number of persons increase.

One of the essential prerequisites needed to make this possible is freedom.[9] Freedom is indispensable to the person, because the person is the free expression and affirmation of value. There is no person without this affirmation of value, and this affirmation is not personal if it isn't free, i.e., if it is not free to come spontaneously from within the person. Individuals, then, need a forced order, imposed from without. Persons, since there is no conflict between them but only a community of interests, need no such imposition. This coincidence of interests is made possible only because of an orientation which is objective, not subjective. The person has the tendency to transcend his own interests. The individual utilizes things and people to advance his own interests. The individual respects only that which is—not that which ought to be. The person respects that which ought to be—and also that which is—if it is as it ought to be. The attempt to change what is to what ought to be is the sum and substance of the person's viewpoint and introduces the element of ethical values to be realized in practice by the person.

✓   ✓   ✓

Romero discusses further his concept of "spirit" in his *Filosofía Contemporánea*.[10] Here he presents us with an historical overview of different attempts at definition which have been suggested in the course of the past two thousand years. He admits at the outset that the term itself is quite difficult to define. One must differentiate between a personal spirit and an objective spirit; one must bear in mind the dynamics of the spirit as well as the lack of agreement concerning the means of grasping the spiritual.[11]

Socrates can perhaps be called the first theoretician of the spirit. His objection to Sophist relativism is the result of his attempt to discover the possibility of objective knowledge and wisdom. He seeks these as a base upon which to erect an absolute morality. His defense of this objectivity would seem to imply that the latter is the predominant characteristic of spiritual essence. But with Socrates too, the dominant note, if not the equivalent of spirit, is reason, a unilateral vision of spirituality.[12]

The distinction between the psyche and the spiritual appears again in the Middle Ages. It was Averroes who, in order to emphasize the distinction, postulated a universal spirit within which particular individuals participated. In other words, spirit within man was but a part or reflection of the One Total Spirit.[13]

The rationalist view of the spirit which would render equivalent knowledge and virtue, science and morality, was to influence human thought for many centuries to come. Perhaps it was natural that this be so. Philosophy at first had investigated the nature of things; only later did it concern itself with the nature of man. Things belong to certain aspects of humanity which are more evident, more easily accessible and observable.

The intellectualistic view of the spirit prevailed in the philosophic realm until Kant appeared on the scene and formulated an entirely different view of the spirit. For Kant, the subject of the cognitive process does not possess an analytical, logical, discriminating instrument with which to penetrate reality, but rather a synthetic reason which creates the object in order to know it; or perhaps it would be more accurate to say, a reason which creates and knows it simultaneously. Ultimate reality is destined to remain unattainable via cognitive means which are inadequate to the task.

As far as the spirit is concerned, philosophers in the romantic tradition, such as Schopenhauer and Bergson, were subsequently to use this historical juncture to tell us what they thought reality is like, because they imagined the human spirit to be possessed of powers of cognition other than the rational.

A slightly different slant to the conception of the spirit is added at the beginning of the 19th century, affirms Romero. Hegel advances the postulate for the first time that side by side with the spirit that resides within us, i.e., the spirit as subjectivity, there exists also the spirit outside us, spirit as objectivity. Law, morality, the State—these are also expressions of the spirit.

Romero refers to Max Scheler as a point of departure for more recent studies. Technical intelligence, one of the elements of the psycho-physical make-up of man, comes closest to spirit and is most often confused with it,—so much so, that spirit is frequently conceived of as the last and most highly developed stage in the evolution of intelligence. Yet there is an enormous difference. Men as well as animals utilize intelligence in order to exist, in order to deal with their environment which appears to them in the shape of things that have to be overcome, or, in short, things which offer resistance. Technical intelligence applies only to these "things—resistances."[14] This process basically amounts to existence. Spirit, on the other hand, views things and objects as devoid of resistance. It contemplates them as pure essences, and projects itself toward them not for the sake of utilizing them, but rather in order to appreciate them for their own sake, as essential manifestations of the structure of the universe. Scheler suggests the term "objectivity" as a dominant trait of the spiritual attitude, to describe the act of projecting oneself toward the object without any thought being given to the individual's center of interest.[15] Technical intelligence, then, is to existence what spirit is to essence. In Scheler's view, spirit is certainly not as sturdy and powerful as the lower forms of being, e.g., the physical and biological. It is weak and delicate since it is the highest form, and consequently has to feed on or "colonize" the lower levels, moulding them to its purposes and spiritualizing them.[16]

The conflict between life and spirit continues. Scheler's optimism points to a spiritualization of life, as indeed does the entire Judeo-Christian tradition. On the other side of the ledger, "Nietzsche, pragmatism and the other vitalist currents . . . affirm life as against spirit."[17] But Romero ends on an optimistic note. "The spirit strives to apprehend essences beyond empirical diversity; it affirms values beyond natural tendencies, egotistical impulses."[18] Spirit thrives on resistance, on opposition. In fact, if resistance were to disappear, spirit would lose its opportunity to assert itself. For spirit is tension and aspiration, rather than an end in itself.

✦ ✦ ✦

Becoming, rather than being, is paramount in Romero, reminding one of Heraclitus and Hegel. The doctrine of "emergent evolution" also comes to mind. The world is characterized by activity, movement, action and interaction. Yet this world is not chaotic nor without meaning. It is structured according to different levels of reality, each level serving as a foundation for the next higher level. Becoming implies "transcendence." By means of transcendence, human beings ascend and project themselves as they strive to achieve the highest realm, the spiritual. As we ascend from one level to the next, we note an increase in the degree of transcendence.

> There is more transcendence in the organic than in the physical, more in the intentional than in the organic, and more in the spiritual than in the merely intentional. Spiritual transcendence represents the apex; there is no higher level; it represents absolute and total transcendence.[19]

It is clear from the above quotation that there are four levels of reality. Each level forms the base and support of

121

the next higher level. Romero first broaches this hierarchical scheme in his *Programa de una filosofía.*[20] These four levels of reality, the physical, the organic, the psychic and the spiritual, are interwoven with two other concepts: transcendence, already referred to, and intentionality. Moreover, beginning with the organic level, each stratum of reality takes root in the order immediately below and "colonizes" it, i.e., subdues and utilizes it. For example, the animal realm colonizes plant life by feeding on it, and this occurs only after both plant and animal life have imposed special forms and patterns upon physical reality for their own benefit.[21] Scheler's influence is quite marked in this respect.

Romero equates "physical" with "inorganic;" "organic" is "pre-intentional psychism;" the psychic itself is mere intentionality. What Romero calls transcendence is assumed to be present as a universal principle at the lowest or inorganic level, although it is difficult of detection. On the organic plane, however, it appears visible, grows more powerful in the psyche or intentional level, and becomes absolute in the spiritual realm.

On the lowest stratum of Romero's hierarchy, i.e., inorganic matter, the quantitative element is at a maximum and the qualitative at a minimum. Nevertheless, even on this plane of reality there is evidence of a coherent, rather than a disordered universe, both in space and time. Any change in the physical world is due to the fact that objects seek to emerge from their present condition in an attempt to find a different, and by implication, a better or "higher" status.

The second level of reality, the organic, depends for its sustenance on the first basic stage. The organic stage consists of two interconnected aspects: the purely organic and the psychic. The vital aspect is, of course, an outgrowth of the purely physical realm within which it is included and hence cannot be entirely divorced therefrom. It is superimposed, so to speak, upon the inorganic, and yet initiates a process of individualization. "The capacity toward individualization is limited in the inorganic sphere; the appearance of life implies, above all, a powerful increase of individualizing energy."[22]

What is meant by "individualization?" "Individualization is particularization, the formation of closed and private nuclei, separate from everything else."[23] Yet paradoxically, the progress of individuality and particularity is at the same time a step forward in the direction of universality, of freedom from confinement within the particular. This is so because a larger measure of individualization carries within itself the potential for a greater radius of action, for increased capacity to project oneself outward toward more varied and more extensive areas of activity.

The animal stage is characterized by a "pre-intentional psychism," as contrasted with "intentional psychism," or intentional consciousness, the exclusive domain of the human being. The animal experiences his world passively, a world composed of a series of conditions or states of being of which it is itself a part, rather than one consisting of objects which are consciously perceived by a subject. The "object" in Romero's sense, is generally anything that has meaning for the subject. In other words, whereas in the "pre-intentional psychic" state the animal merely experiences existence without specific referral to a subjective point of reference, i.e., an ego, on the intentional level, by contrast, man is conscious of himself as a perceiving and acting subject who converts vague and amorphous states or media into specific, well-defined objects toward which he is to react. For example, an intense pain may be merely experienced without having any cognition take place, or else, it may be objectified and perceived, i.e., become the object which stimulates an intentional act. Intentionality, or psyche, thus distinguishes man from animal, and characterizes the third stage in Romero's structure. The characteristic of man is to perceive, to *objectify,* to be conscious of a *subject-object* relationship, and to judge accordingly.[24]

In intentional behavior, an act, after having completed its trajectory, so to speak, toward the object of the subject's intentions, returns to the subject in "boomerang" fashion.

Acts are useful or useless, agreeable or disagreeable, etc., since it is the subject that is the end and purpose of all activity. This is essentially what links man to nature. Man is here identified by Romero as the "natural" man who behaves according to the law of particularism, rather than universality. Even when man acts for the good of his family or his social group, he is still acting within the framework of the "natural."

At the stage of intentionality, or psyche, transcendence reaches a higher level. Life "colonizes" matter, psyche "colonizes" life, and spirit (which characterizes the fourth and highest stage) "colonizes" the psyche. As has been pointed out, each level must depend for its existence upon the one which precedes it.

It is in the fourth and final stage, the spiritual, where transcendence has the opportunity to soar to its greatest heights, where man's self-centered intentionality disappears, and human action completes its trajectory toward the object and *stays there* without returning to the subject.[25] The world of the spirit is devoid of utilitarian motives. Action is divested of its particularistic nature and, instead, assumes a *universalistic* intentionality.

For Romero, the concept "spirit" does not partake of a supernatural, mysterious character. "Spirit" is human, peculiarly human. The spiritual act is performed for "the other," not for the "self." The "natural" man, in contrast to the "spiritual" man, has not yet raised himself, has not "transcended" to universality. The ego is still the main center.

In short, the individual views objects from the standpoint of their use to him. He "colonizes," "enslaves," and "devours" them. Objects exist in order to be exploited; objectivities are created only to be subordinated to his immediate goals. Intentional acts are projected toward these objectivities; within these acts a return to the subject is envisaged.

In contrast, the spiritual act is characterized by a complete absence of such return. "The self is concerned with the objectivities for what they are in themselves."[26] Just as there is a distinction between the spiritual and the intentional, there is likewise a difference to be encountered between the intentional and the next lower level of reality, i.e., pre-intentional psychism. The latter adapts the individual to his environment, and also vice-versa, in a partial sense. The individual in this case is nothing more than organic life. By contrast, intentional psychism, makes of the individual more than just an organic entity. He now operates in a world which he can recognize and within which he can experience free choice; he can now create culture, something he could not do on the purely vital level. He can now live in both worlds: nature *and* culture, and predominantly in the latter.

The spirit is but the end result of intentionality or intentional psychism. Intentional psychism in turn, is based on pre-intentional psychism. The animal, as has been pointed out, existing on the level of pre-intentional psychism does not create objectivities. Man, who operates on the level of intentional psychism, does. Objectivization, i.e., the creation of objects or objectivities is thus a key concept in Romero. At the moment that intentionality or intentional psychism objectivizes, it brings into being the duality, subject-object. One cannot exist without the other. The self is the subject and the center of intentional psychism. The self is, then, a being that creates objects, grasps and relates them. The spirit can be said to exist in embryonic form within intentional psychism.

As one moves up the scale of reality, e.g., from the realm of the inorganic to that of the organic, one also advances "from the more to the less determined, from fatalism to freedom."[27] At the highest level, that of spiritual activity, one expects to find a maximum of freedom. Yet man is not capable of purely spiritual acts. He is also a natural man. At best he is a dual being; mere intentionality combines with spirit within him.[28] The self, then, exists between two levels, or rather, it can be said to oscillate between the level at which it performs intentional acts, characterized by objective projection and subjective return, and the higher plane in which no such return is expected. Insofar as pre-intentional psychic activity is concerned, i.e., the level of the purely biological, there is no projection at all.

At times, the self may develop into a group of selves, a "we," rather than an "I." In this case, the intentionality, although enlarged and therefore superior, is still particular. The subjective return of the act is still in force. The act still takes place within the realm of "nature," rather than "spirit," since nature is that segment of reality whose components act with reference to themselves. An act which takes place within the spiritual realm is defined by its disinterestedness. For "spirit" refers to "those subjects and acts projected totally toward objectivities, with no other motive on the part of the subjects than to yield themselves toward the other (i.e., the object which exists or that which is valuable, whatever the case may be)."[29]

What, then, are the distinguishing characteristics of the spirit? Among the chief traits is that of absolute objectivity. When the subject performs a merely intentional act, he bestows upon it a highly subjective quality. The object is "something for the subject."[30] In the case of a spiritual act, the interest shown toward the object in question is "disinterested," i.e., it is not governed by any interest peculiar to the subject, or redounding to the subject's benefit. On the contrary, the subject is interested in the existence of the object for its own sake.

A second trait of the spirit is its universality. The spirit aspires toward totality in all directions—"cognitive, ethic, aesthetic."[31] A third element is freedom, i.e., in the sense of furnishing a setting within which the particularism in man is encouraged to give way to universalistic tendencies.

The spirit is also characterized by unity. This is the case when, e.g., basic ethical premises are recognized and the subjects experience a certain identity in following the dictates of these premises. Compare this with the divergence and conflict caused by particular interests which govern purely intentional acts.

Respect and "disinterested" interest are also essential. The spirit respects and is interested in everything. The arts and sciences are an outgrowth of this type of interest. Two additional traits are limitless responsibility and self-awareness. But the most important characteristic of the spiritual act is that of absolute transcendence which involves a total projection of one's self toward the "other," without the possibility of the "subjective return."[32] The spiritual level is its own end; transcendence reaches its maximum. There is no higher plane of existence. To cite an example: In the pursuit of knowledge, the individual is interested in a given object only because of the practical benefits that can accrue to him. By contrast, the person is interested in the object, for the sake of the object itself, without consideration as to its eventual usefulness to him.

Historicity must also be considered as a necessary ingredient of the spirit. Spiritual acts have an historic source and represent an historical conquest. History offers instances of individuals or groups that have in the past initiated certain spiritual attitudes unknown before. These groups or people were instrumental in educating others in the task of adopting these attitudes.

The bond between historicity and time is undeniable. The two are intertwined and inseparable. The transition in philosophy from fixedness and rigorous identity to temporalism represents a moving away from the position of classical rationalism and, consequently, a closer approximation toward reality.[33] Whereas non-temporal 17th century Rationalism corresponded to the scientific conception of the mechanized world, the metaphysical role of time now goes hand in hand with contemporary scientific views. Present-day conceptions of the atom and of the physical universe, for example, involve temporal or historicist interpretations. Romero's principle of universal transcendence is actualized temporally, i.e., historically. In short, historicity is the result of the temporal channeling of transcendence. It is easier to perceive historicity in the organic than in the inorganic realm. Human historicity depends on the duality basic to man, namely, the confluence of intentional structure and spirituality.[34] Cultural transformation is effected through community historicity. The individual is made to feel that he plays an active role as a member of the group in the process of making history. This would explain the emergence of the concepts "left," "right" and "center", concepts which perform a necessary function in history-making, and which are to be viewed as broad, cultural categories, rather than merely political designations. The "left" and the "right" represent innovating and conserving tendencies, respectively; the "center" is merely an attempt at conciliation. In other words, "leftist tendencies represent the need to surpass what has been achieved; they prevent the community and the culture from stagnating, ossifying and perishing historically. Rightist tendencies, on the other hand, prevent the culture and the community from dissolving or falling over a precipice by insisting on the value of what has been achieved."[35]

Historicity, then, consists of both innovation and conservation. Both are involved in the progress of man, community and culture. Innovation concentrates on history in the making; conservation concerns itself with history that has been completed.

The tensions and conflicts created as a result of man's duality, i.e., the interaction between mere intentionality and spirituality, leave their impact upon the historicity of both the individual and the group. Spiritual acts broaden man's field of action. An historical task is performed when the spiritual principle triumphs, i.e., when it colonizes the non-spiritual. Communal historicity is attained when the spiritual principle establishes a norm which will eventually tend to promote a higher average level of behavior for the community. The concept of historicity, as applied to culture, can best be illustrated by reference to the question of value. In this respect, there is an attempt at continual apprehension, application and refinement of values. Great historical periods, e.g., have been known for the "world view" which they represented, i.e., their critical vision and evaluation of life and of the world. World views, with their temporal character, are therefore elements in the historicity of culture.[36]

The spiritual subject is not only responsible to himself as a person, but also to other persons who are conceived to be of equal value. Hence, responsibility also, must not be lost sight of as a necessary trait of the spirit.

Reality, for Romero, is activity. For him there are no permanent essences, or fixed unchanging realities. All is action and interaction. Yet all this activity should not be thought of as chaotic and disorganized. The key concept of transcendence needs to be grasped in order to see that activity grows, proceeds and develops in orderly fashion. As a matter of fact, transcendence is a concept which is never too clearly defined by Romero. It implies projection toward others, emergence from one's own confines; it is present everywhere, either in potential or embryonic form, or else it is realizing itself. The world is animated by this positive, creative impulse. In fact, there would be no cosmos without it. And man, as part of the cosmos, possesses within himself the potential for acting as a transcendent and creative totality.

In contrast to transcendence, Romero posits immanence, which he defines as "confinement within one's own particular reality."[37] The subject is a prisoner of his private interests. In transcendence one can validly say that the subject not only possesses his acts but is possessed by them. For transcendence amounts to a giving of oneself, a going out from oneself, yet, at the same time, maintaining one's own identity. One does not cease to be after transcendence has been attained.

Freedom can be said to exist as a function of, and in direct ratio to the measure of transcendence. For example, the animal, or the purely biological individual, is limited in his action: his situations are rigid and immediate. The intentional individual who is capable of partial transcendence operates in a realm which has far more possibilities, so that he enjoys a degree of autonomy unknown to the animal. As we ascend to the highest level it becomes obvious that the absolute transcendence, characteristic of the spiritual person carries with it even greater freedom. Naturally, regressions can be anticipated. For just as the subject may step out of himself and return again to himself, so similarly, can transcendence be halted in its trajectory and become immanent on occasion, in which case it is known as restricted transcendence in contrast to total or absolute transcendence.

The individual can also be said to be characterized in terms of a centripetal force. Essentially, the world around him is viewed from the vantage point of his own center of interest. Everything flows inward toward him, toward the center.

The person, on the other hand is identified with a centrifugal force. The person is outgoing; everything within him flows outward *toward* objects and people.

To phrase it somewhat differently, utilizing two of Romero's favorite terms: the psyche which predominates in the individual turns its attention inward, a process described as "immanentization." This, in contrast to the spirit, which guides the person, and which prefers "transcendence" as a means of expressing itself. Transcendence seems to be equivalent to an impulse which always moves forward, outward and upward, in continually aspiring fashion.[38]

To go the other way, i.e., in a downward "immanentist" direction, would amount to subsuming value under being; the spirit would be subsidiary to the psyche, the psychic would be a subheading of the biological which, in turn, would be a subdivision of the material.

The individual, then, is immanentist; he ignores or looks down upon values, or else he bends them to his purpose. He utilizes other individuals. By contrast, the very essence of the person is to transcend toward values. His generous impulses, like life itself, cause him to "spill over," so to speak, giving rather than taking. From this perspective, being and value become fused into one.

The human person, representing lofty ethical objectives to be cultivated and respected, has the best chance of developing in our Western culture, more so in spite of periodic drawbacks than in any other culture. To renounce this possibility of development is equivalent to descending to the level of the beast. And to show that he is no "ivory tower" philosopher, Romero warns that such a descent into chaos would amount to repeating "the tragic experience of Hiroshima."[39]

A refreshing note is injected at this point. Romero, in contrast to the excessive confidence and closed-mindedness of the Positivist school, writes: ". . . let the reader remember all my 'maybes' and 'perhapses.' My task is not to dogmatize, nor am I accustomed to present my possibilities as certainties. I don't intend to surrender a right . . . which does not exclude certain inconveniences: the right to doubt."[40] This note in Romero's thinking is perhaps best summarized in the concluding lines of his essay on "Scepticism and relativism:" ". . . . let us always hope to attain the truth; let us always have little hope of possessing it."[41]

Romero's study of the history of philosophy led him to adopt a position of suspicion toward closed systems and to assume a constantly problematical attitude. He insisted on the importance of unhampered study, on the tentative and provisional quality of conclusions arrived at, and on the need and willingness to modify continually, i.e., to make and unmake systems and opinions. However, it should be pointed out that he was painfully aware of the fact that the philosopher and the historian of ideas are often "culture bound," whether they realize it or not, i.e., they manifest the bias of their own philosophical training, in spite of their well-intentioned attempt at so-called objectivity.[42]

✓   ✓   ✓

In connection with the concepts of immanence and transcendence, Romero discusses two notions which have been associated with reality: structure and evolution. In either case transcendence is involved. Structure is not merely an aggregate of individual parts: what is implied in the concept is the existence of a potential or possibility within the parts which, when realized, results in something more than a mere arithmetic sum of those parts.

This potential which implies envisioning qualitative, not merely quantitative change, functions only if one is willing to replace the atomistic concept by this structural interpretation. When the potential realizes itself into what it was meant to be, it simply illustrates the notion of transcendence so dear to Romero. Structure and transcendence complement each other. " . . . structure adds something that was not evident in the parts . . ." "The parts transcend in a certain way once the structure is formed."[43] Structure then, is a *Gestalt,* the end result of individual parts which have transcended themselves into a new synthesis.

If structure is associated with space, evolution can be said to be connected with time. Evolution or development is a transcending in a temporal sense, in which the entity projects itself into the future. Unfortunately, evolution, one of the great romantic intuitions, under the influence of Spencer and Darwin, became mechanized, rationalized, "immanentized."[44]

It is at this point that Romero takes issue with the mechanistic conception of reality which, he claims, ignores the transcendental impetus involved in the process of change. According to the mechanistic interpretation, only spatial distribution is involved, i.e., elements are altered with respect to their distribution, but they remain essentially identical. The temporal factor has been removed completely. This mechanistic view, identified with the doctrine of rationalism, condemns all transcendence as being an illusion. If elements remain identical, then the principle emphasized is one of immanence. In Romero's view, space is related to immanence, and time is directly associated with transcendence. Rationalistic and mechanistic interpretations of reality have sinned against the latter.

Reference has already been made to the four levels of reality: the physical or inorganic, the vital or organic, intentional psychism, and spirit. The degree of transcendence increases as one ascends from one level to the next. At the

132

lowest level, namely, the inorganic, transcendence seems least visible. At the highest level, the spiritual, it attains its absolute. The reverse can be said for immanence. This decreases in degree and force as one ascends. In other words, immanence decreases as transcendence increases. Yet immanence serves a purpose. It is a sort of matrix out of which transcendence emerges. "The function of immanence would seem to be the formation of centers of transcendence, or perhaps, the storing up of latent transcendence which is actualized once adequate channels become available."[45] Furthermore, the degree of transcendence is not increased at a uniform rate. There is far more transcendence at the top than at the lower levels of reality, e.g., more at the organic than at the very bottom or physical level, more on the intentional plane than on the organic, and certainly far more at the spiritual level. There is no higher level than spiritual transcendence; it is itself total and absolute.

Transcendence, then, is achieved at the expense of immanence. Actually, Romero seems to be uncertain at this point. One may well ask: Is immanence a separate entity to be acted upon and converted by transcendence, or is it, instead, a sheaf of potential, dormant transcendencies which are merely waiting for the opportune moment to be tipped off by action and experience in order to awaken and realize themselves to the utmost? Romero seems to favor the second interpretation.[46]

The concept of transcendence is intimately related to Romero's theory of value. Transcendence determines the degree of value. It is through transcendence that we achieve value. In fact, there is a positive correlation between the two. The organic is therefore more valuable than the physical, and the intentional more so than the organic, because the respective planes are like platforms which make possible new and more active forms of transcendence. Consequently, each form of transcendence has its own value. Values are both relative and absolute. Spiritual values are absolute, because it is only in the spirit that absolute transcendence is possible.

Through man the world can attain to the maximum degree of "disinterestedness." Far from agreeing with Heidegger's position that death is man's destiny, Romero argues that the destiny of man is value. The end of all existence is the realization of value. "To be is to transcend," and transcendence is co-existent with value.

Romero thus affirms the metaphysical dignity of man. The upward path assumed by the universe culminates in man. The destiny of man is the very destiny of the world itself. It is through man that the world can free itself of its limitations. Romero's dynamic optimism and faith in man's possibilities place him in the ranks of those who have always fought for justice and liberty on all fronts.

One question still remains, a question which may conceivably leave us perplexed. If Romero implies that his formula, individual-person, runs paralled and is akin to a series of other dualities, such as nature-spirit and determinism-freedom, then one may ask with some justification: What exactly is the nature of this spirit that liberates man from nature? Is it, as Rodríguez-Alcalá asks, "an immaterial substance, active, creative, incorruptible, imperishable?" Romero seems to shy away from attributing a substantive quality to spirit. It would appear that spirit is something built into the structure of Romero's scaffolding. It is program, plan and purpose. It is the "role we play."

Rodríguez-Alcalá quotes Ortega y Gasset in this connection, and asserts that both the Spanish and Argentine philosophers deny the substantiveness of the ego.

"Man is ... something that has neither corporal nor spiritual reality; he is a program ... of what he is not as yet, but aspires to be ..."[47]

Whence, therefore, comes this spirit that causes us to "play a certain role" and not another? Where does this "program" come from? Who or what causes it to appear at times, or to slumber on other occasions? Can the appearance of the spiritual act of the person, as opposed to the

134

purely intentional act of the individual, be said to appear suddenly *ex nihilo,* without cause? This would seem to be a vulnerable spot in the impressive edifice erected by Romero in his attempt to combat the deterministic thesis which denies freedom to man—a thesis characteristic of the Positivist empiricism which swept the continent at the close of the 19th century.

✓ ✓ ✓

Value, then, varies in direct ratio to transcendence, i.e., the greater the transcendence, the higher the value and the higher the reality. "Value is equivalent to the degree of transcendence and, consequently, the measure of the actual reality of being."[48] Romero rejects the distinction often made between subjective and objective values, or between that which is determined by the attitudes of the subject and the quality which is superimposed upon acts. Instead, values are divided into spiritual or absolute, and non-spiritual or relative. At this point, Romero introduces additional terminology. He affirms that there are differences in the magnitude and dignity of values. Obviously, relative values are never quite equal to absolute values in magnitude and dignity. However, when Romero speaks of value in terms of dignity, i.e., the greater the dignity, the higher the value, he does not seem to add to the clarity of his exposition, since the term "dignity" is itself value-laden. Elsewhere,[49] he speaks of dignity and its relationship to the "magnitude of transcendence." Transcendence, dignity and value, then, seem to vary with one another in direct ratio. The reasoning, though, appears circular. Spiritual values are absolute because absolute transcendence is to be found only in the spirit, i.e., it is only in spiritual acts that the subject can arrive at absolute values.

It is conceivable that a non-spiritual subject may produce a spiritual creation, and a spiritual act may yield a non-spiritual product. This is so because of the difference between intent and result. "Transcendence for the subject consists in the nature of the intention, not in the quality of the result, while the cultural product is a result ... (which is) inde-

135

pendent of the subjective intentions that produced it."[50] The merely intentional subject achieves relative values. He can arrange a hierarchy of evaluation and compare them. However, he cannot compare relative and absolute values, because he cannot apprehend the latter. This can be done only by the spiritual subject.

Since there is a direct relationship between value and transcendence, it follows that relative value is indicative of incomplete transcendence, i.e., a transcendence which has not freed itself completely from immanence. When transcendence reaches the level at which it functions absolutely free of any trace of immanence, it can be said to have created absolute value which is the exclusive domain of the spirit. This also coincides with a moving away from subjectivity in the direction of absolute objectivity.

Romero's formulation applies to cognitive as well as ethical values. Cognitive apprehending implies apprehending knowledge of an object by a subject. Cognitive value therefore relates to objective apprehension. In accordance with the directives which Romero establishes, it follows that cognitive value which is relative occurs in merely intentional acts, whereas absolute cognitive value is to be found in the domain of spiritual acts of knowledge.

One must separate carefully the interrelated threads which connect value, act and knowledge. In intentional knowledge, the correct apprehension of the object is sought because it is of interest to the subject. In the case of spiritual knowledge, this correct apprehension is sought for its own sake. Moreover, it is in the very nature of the spirit to know all there is to know, to know all the parts of the whole, to know the ultimate to the very depths.

A distinction must be made at this point. If the cognitive act apprehends the object faithfully, then the knowledge is said to be true. However, the apprehension may be erroneous without detracting from the value of the act itself. Again, one must distinguish between intention and result; value is associated in this case with the subject's intention. In other words, a spiritual act of knowledge may lead to a false result whereas a non-spiritual act, i.e., one performed on the purely intentional level may conceivably produce a true result. The first act would, nevertheless, possess absolute cognitive value whereas the second would not. In short, absolute cognitive value is derived from the subject's intention; it does not depend upon the truth uncovered in the result. However, when it is a question of objectified knowledge, the element of truth cannot be discounted.[51] In the latter case, the subject's intentions are set aside; value falls on the truth instead.

To sum up: many acts which are transcendent from the standpoint of intentionality, and consequently possessed of absolute value, may conceivably fail. On the other hand, there may be acts which are not based on purely spiritual motives and which are therefore only relatively valuable which, nevertheless, may produce results that are valuable in an absolute sense.

Spirit can never be satisfied with the cognitive attitude, because the latter is merely concerned with what is. Spirit which is pure transcendence engages in acts which reveal ethical value. "Absolute ethical value exists only in the absolutely transcendent act, that is, in the spiritual act."[52]

To sum up: the greater the magnitude of the transcendence which is released and allowed to operate freely, the greater the degree of ethical activity, i.e., the person's duty or obligation. Absolute ethical acts are directed without any concern for the relationship which these acts bear to the subject who perpetrates them. Absolute ethical value corresponds to absolute transcendence; the acts in question, when directed toward human beings, amount to an absolute obligation.

An apparent inconsistency appears at this point. Value in Romero's view is not subjective. "We accept the objectivity of value . . ."[53] But then he appears to contradict himself when he asserts in the same sentence: "Value for us is not a special quality superimposed upon acts, nor is it something exclusively subjective, insofar as it is determined by evaluating attitudes of the subject . . ."[54] For cannot "a special quality superimposed upon acts" be interpreted to mean an objective entity existing in isolation, divorced from subjective preferences, and selected only when the subject is inclined to do so? In an earlier work, *Filosofía de la persona*, as Augusto Salazar Bondy[55] correctly points out, Romero writes: "Values are certain qualities whose essence consists purely in being valued, in showing a certain dignity objectively and without reference to that which in each case satisfies natural impulse, our individual, transitory desire."[56]

It would appear then that in this particular case, not only is there a contradiction between one work and another, but also within the same work, as the two quotations from *Teoría del hombre* reveal.

✓ ✓ ✓

Romero analyzes the causes of the world's present crisis in an essay entitled "El Positivismo y la crisis"[57] and concludes that it is chiefly the lack of a widely held constellation of common beliefs and convictions concerning man and his destiny, that is responsible for his predicament.

Those who assert that the crisis is merely economic in origin should remember that man's psychological motivations are basic; that all factors, including the economic one, are reacted to within the framework of a complex cluster of beliefs, evaluations, propensities, habits and points of view. One's attitude toward the approach of death, e.g., is governed by one's convictions. What is basic, then, is man's configuration of beliefs, what he thinks of life and of the world; not the data to be found in the world's events or even within his own physical being, but rather the way he elaborates and interprets the data, and this he does in accordance with his psychological make-up.

It lies within the very nature of man to possess a point of view, a value system, a conception of the world—all of these subject to variability due to differences in temperament, social group, class structure, etc.

"At times the presence of the desirable does not even provoke desire ... The decision to fight for what one does not possess, and even the sense of experiencing its absence

138

violently, as an intolerable void . . . these stem principally from psychic reasons . . ."[58]

An historical epoch, too, especially a great and outstanding one, is possessed of a viewpoint, a *Weltanschauung*. Perhaps it is precisely because of its special conception of the world that the epoch is great. Moreover, the power, grandeur and influence of this conception is attested to by virtue of the fact that the vast majority of people living during this age is simply permeated with its spirit without being conscious thereof. Only a small, distinguished minority can perceive the quality of its principles.[59]

During the Middle Ages, western civilization possessed a universal conception of the world. The Renaissance replaced this with a different set of principles, and ushered in the Modern Age, a process which was to be concluded in the 18th century. Rationalism and empiricism made their peace, the mechanist conception of the universe exuded confidence and acquired powerful prestige, especially after Newton, and the belief in the inevitability of human progress emerged triumphant.

Romero continues to follow the philosophical trajectory. He points to the eruption of Romanticism as a protest against the Enlightenment, only to be succeeded by the appearance of Positivism which was to dominate the intellectual climate of the second half of the 19th century. Comtian positivism or that of J.S. Mill was a continuation of the empiricist tradition; the scientific-materialist current had much in common with rationalism. Within Positivism, then, were to be found the two principal streams, characteristic of the Modern Age: empiricism and rationalism.

But it was Darwinian evolution that made of Positivism more than just a revised and enlarged version of the Enlightenment. Within the latter there had been no provision made for the merely organic world. On the other hand, the theory of evolution not only gave additional substantiation to the belief in progress, but also assigned a causative and rational interpretation to the world of organic phenomena. The biological sciences were now adduced to support faith in progress. In fact, man, history and culture could be explained via the laws of biological evolution.[60] Positivism, then, represented the culminating point of the modern world view; its conviction was mechanist and scientific in its emphasis. Reality, as conceived of by Darwin and Spencer, simply had to move forward inexorably, a process which was based on the mechanical play of natural forces. Positivism was based on a "faith in the perfectibility of man, in limitless progress, in the future."[61]

And here Romero arrives at the key concept of his thesis, namely, his assertion as to the reason for the present world crisis. The new philosophy rejected Positivism. Strictly mechanist and narrowly interpreted Darwinian formulas were severely criticized and brought into question; inevitable progress became the target of searching sceptics; the pendulum as it had done so often on other occasions, was ready to swing again to the other extreme. The "bankruptcy of science" brought about agonizing disillusion; some sought solace in a return to the traditional, institutionalized forms of religion; others transferred their allegiance to a corrosive nihilism, or else, rendered worship to the cult of the immediate and the momentary. The appearance of waves of unbridled nationalism may also, according to Romero, be said to have been an expression of this loss of faith in man's destiny.[62]

The present world crisis is but a stage in the evolution of Western culture. The crisis does not represent the decadence or failure of Western civilization, as Spengler, e.g., would have us believe. It is merely the expression of an absence of convictions, ideas and aspirations of our age. Beliefs help one to live, because in order to live it is necessary to be anchored to a psychologically secure base.

The fact is that the so-called Modern Age of Western culture has entered a critical phase. Romero maintains that it is fundamentally important for man to have ideas and beliefs which will sustain him. Living means acting, behaving and reacting against a background of psychological security. The trouble is that our Modern Age lacks these

140

beliefs, this inner sense of security. Our crisis stems from the fact that we are now in a transitional stage. One set of beliefs has just been ended for us, and the next one has not yet made its appearance. Contemporary man is without *terra firma*. He has lost his coherent and consistent *Weltanschauung;* he has been divested of his blind faith in science, in man's perfectibility and unending progress.

In spite of it all, however, Romero ends on an optimistic note. Criticism of Positivism should not obscure the fact that the latter did, after all, project the notion of man's advance. In this connection Romero quotes the Uruguayan philosopher, Carlos Vaz Ferreira, to the effect that, strange as it seems, man's spiritual progress surpasses his material achievements, and that "morality has advanced in history at a more rapid rate than have his technical accomplishments."[63]

Fully aware of the fact that attempts to draw a parallel between historical movements have their dangers, Romero nevertheless asserts that Romanticism and Renaissance had some traits in common. Both were periods of revolt and transition ("El itinerario de la filosofía contemporánea y la crisis."[64]) The Renaissance, stressing the primacy of individual man, rebelled against the authority and tradition of the Middle Ages and represented the transition between the Medieval and the Modern Age. Romanticism was a rebellion against the 18th century Rationalist conception of the world, characteristic of the Modern Age, and also served as a transitional stage between the latter and what was to follow.

If Romanticism with its emphasis upon instinct, fantasy, emotion and intuition, with its affinity for religion and art rather than science, can be said to be a protest against the alliance of rationalism and empiricism, then the appearance of Positivism, the reaction against the Romantic protest, can be considered to be an attempt to restore the Modern Period. This restoration was marked by an emphasis on a science which followed in the footsteps of 18th century materialism, to which was added a Darwinism that attempted to apply a biological mechanistic formula to the earth's phenomena. In typical Hegelian fashion, the contemporary reaction to the Positivistic "restoration" of the Modern Age was not long in making its appearance—a reaction with Romantic overtones, but one which was much more precise and scientific than Romanticism and also, at the same time, more profound and complex then Darwinism or Spencerianism. This higher synthesis has not yet utilized or exhausted all of its possibilities.

It is typical of all entities to struggle against narrow confinement, to wish to reach out, expand and change, to "out-do" themselves, as it were. This point of view is closely linked to the Romantic notion of growth and development, to evolution, to *Gestalt*. The total structure always makes for the addition of something which was not evident in the individual parts originally, but which nevertheless has its roots or foundation in those parts, in latent form to be sure, but which functions in full bloom, thanks to the formation of the new *Gestalt*. Once again, Romero refers to the two concepts, structuralism and transcendence, which he attempts to correlate. Both have their antecedents and inspiration in the Romantic movement. The universe is animated by an inner impulse which creates higher forms and makes it possible for new goals to emerge and evolve. *Gestalt* acquires meaning only when considered as creative transcendence, or in short, when the effect is superior to the cause.

Romero's transcendence runs counter to scientific mechanism which found its inspiration in rationalism. Scientific and philosophic materialism did not provide for transcendence, and thereby destroyed all possibility of authentic change. Rationalism's position was one of "immanentization": immanence of knowledge (Cartesianism), or religious belief (Protestantism), and of power (the doctrine of Natural Law). The individual was the sole source and depository of knowledge, belief and sovereignty. What had been initiated by Hobbes was brought to culmination by Darwin. Transcendence was completely suppressed by the law of identity.

The statement A=A is an affirmation of immanence. The principle of becoming is ruled out. Romero's advocacy of a dynamic, changing, transcending notion implies that "A" may actually contain ingredients within itself which make it something more than the actual "A."[65] But the fact is that this law of identity ignores a vital gap which must be spanned. To illustrate: Water is the result of hydrogen plus oxygen, only after certain latent possibilities in either have been actualized under certain conditions. The whole, as already noted, is greater than the sum of its parts.

In short, the Modern Age which turned its back on Medieval transcendence, substituted instead universal immanentism. Transcendence, or "projecting outward," was replaced by "turning inward" upon oneself. All vestiges of transcendence had been removed; everything was reduced to matter and mechanical movement. Romero points to the field of psychology as an example. Influenced by scientific conceptions, psychological atomism and association were used to explain behavior. But phenomena cannot be broken down simply into small particles, argues Romero. There is far more involved. There is a bridge which rises up above the chasm in which the individual parts find themselves: a structure, a whole. It is by means of transcendence that we appreciate and understand the totality that was meant to be.

Immanentism has to be and, in fact, is being replaced by transcendence. The narrowly mechanistic, the static and the rationalistic, moor man to the immediate; the transcendental releases him, makes him project, reach out and overreach himself. The physical sciences as well as psychology suffered from an atomistic interpretation as long as they were bound by immanentization.[66] Transcendence brought them into line with *Gestalt* or structuralism.

The crisis has been overcome in philosophy. The concepts of transcendence, structuralism, organicism and evolution—all of them products of Romantic intuition—which had been either shunted aside, mechanized, or rationalized, have now been renewed and incorporated within more critical and rigorous formulas, in consonance with the latest developments in scientific and metaphysical research.

However, in the realm of socio-political values, the crisis is still very acute. This is so because the orientation is still atomistic. This is the crisis of intellectualism, activism and individualism, the three outstanding characteristics of our Western culture.[67] What is needed is for the individual to become a person, and in Romero's terminology, project himself toward value, i.e., toward that which "ought to be." Western man will continue in crisis as long as he is unable to find new opportunities for creativity. His individualism is frustrated because he has not yet discovered a form of political organization that would reconcile in a satisfactory manner his need for planning and his desire for freedom. Intellectually, he has yet to construct a world view which will adequately support his convictions and value system. From the activist standpoint, he must now look for new worlds to conquer, new potentially creative horizons. He will continue to suffer until, on all of the above fronts, he can *objectify* his dynamism, until he can become more of a "person."

In connection with his discussion of the crisis experienced by the Western world, Romero compares our culture with those of India and China. The comparison serves to highlight the contrast between the position of man in occidental as opposed to oriental culture. The individual in both Asiatic cultures tends to transcend his finite state and aspire toward a fusion with the infinite. In the case of India, he merges with the cosmos; in Chinese culture he becomes one with social or racial totality in the form of the national community.

The occidental man, on the other hand, values his own individuality above all else. If he strives to achieve transcendence, it is for the purpose of enriching his being and attaining a greater measure of spirituality. In contrast to the passivity which distinguishes oriental culture, Western man is active and voluntaristic. As a result of his efforts, the culture which he produces is likewise dynamic. None of the characteristics of Western culture, namely, individualism, activism and intellectualism, can satisfactorily resolve the dilemma in which it finds itself. Individualism, without the corrective force of transcendence, deteriorates into excessive particularism and egoism; individual freedom has not come to terms in adequate fashion with the need for effective planning for social welfare. Intellectualism is being challenged by irrational forces and has not met the challenge satisfactorily. Activism is looking for new worlds to conquer and finds itself frustrated because it doesn't find any; besides, in too many cases it has degenerated into political violence. The Occident wishes to westernize the rest of the world; unfortunately, the rest of the world refuses to be westernized. The crisis, then, has served to prevent the individual from creatively objectivizing his dynamic spirituality; it has prevented him from becoming a person.

✓ ✓ ✓

In his chapter on "Culture,"[68] Romero distinguishes between objective culture and cultural life. By objective culture is meant all that which man has created and which is substantial and autonomous, i.e., which has a relatively separate existence apart from the creator. Cultural life, on the other hand, involves the life which man lives, surrounded as he is by the very objects of his creation. Culture, then, embraces all human activity, its products and its forms of behavior.

These two phases cannot, of course, be separated artificially. What man finds in his environment, or what is referred to as objective culture, is the result of human creativity. Man creates culture and then proceeds to live within it. Rarely can this creative process be said to be devoid of the influence of the group, e.g., in the case of law, language and customs. Even in the case of a talented individual who contributes a so-called original creation, it cannot be denied that the collective influence or pressure of a social group, no matter how subtle and barely perceptible, will make itself felt in some shape or manner. In fact, in some cases one receives the impression that the creator or inventor of a cultural product is but "the interpreter of an intuition or a social sentiment."[69]

Culture, then, is the result of man's propensity to objectify. Man places his stamp upon that with which he comes in contact; he produces and changes. A stone, e.g., becomes a paperweight when placed on one's desk.[70] It is now a cultural object because it has acquired a new meaning. A curious paradox becomes evident at this point. In our efforts to preserve "nature" i.e., what is supposedly "pristine," "pure," and "untouched," we must culturalize it. This is illustrated in man's attempts to preserve the natural beauties of forests, to protect wild life, and to care for our national parks. To stretch the point even further everything that man places in reference to himself falls within the realm of cultural objectification. Indeed, "in order to discover nature which is unaffected by culture, one would have to fly to the stars,"[71] and even this statement can now be called into question in view of our activities in space. Cultural creation implies activity: either voluntary or as a response to a stimulus. An emotional reaction may conceivably result in the formation of an attitude toward an object; in this sense it would act as a culturalizing agent upon that object. The only human activity which does not culturalize the object is the process of knowing. For knowing does not alter the object; it merely inquires into it. However, the result of this activity namely, knowledge, is what constitutes a storehouse of culture.

An object of culture must have an autonomous existence. After it is "born," it must acquire an independent existence. It is ejected, so to speak, from the parent, and becomes common property. Moreover, although a cultural object must have a material base in order to exist, the latter is not the principal reality. What is more important is the psychological ingredient involved. For example, a chair or a table is precisely what it is, not because of what it is made of, but rather, because of the purpose for which it has been constructed. The inference which follows is clear: every cultural object is worth something: it can be referred to or conceived of in terms of a value.

A dual process, then, can be said to take place. On the one hand, man humanizes the non-human; he culturalizes untouched nature. On the other, this objective culture is an externalization of what man carries within himself, a projection of his inner reality.

But this is not the only dual process. Man perceives the need for something; he feels or judges that it ought to be. As a result he brings it forth. This is the impulse emanating from within the individual. But now the cultural product must be made public. The community must give its sanction, a sanction ardently desired by the creator. This is the force exerted from the outside upon the individual.

Moreover, not only does man create culture; culture exercises its influence upon man, and can be said to create him.[72] Language, literature, the arts, develop sensitivities as well as the power to think. Religion satisfies man's needs and provides a vehicle for expressing his yearnings. Institutions, agencies, rules and regulations, control his conduct. Knowledge enriches his life. On the other hand, man may lose part of his cultural heritage either through his own fault or that of others. Objective culture, then, influences man in two ways: 1. It guides, educates and humanizes; 2. It dominates, imposes, demands and coerces.

Man and culture are two inseparable terms; neither can be conceived of in isolation, i.e., divorced from the other. When the individual objectivizes, he realizes what the object is for, and thereby establishes in accordance with his intentionality the bases for a human culture. He makes his cultural world; he assigns a value to his object, a value which ascends in the hierarchy of values to the degree that man is able to transcend and go beyond his immediate interests. Not only is culture unthinkable if considered apart from man; values also are inconceivable, apart from culture. And as man creates culture and value, the forms whereby these express themselves manifest a tendency to acquire a separate existence, independent of the individual or group that have brought them into being. Once created, they become part and parcel of the collective heritage; they belong to humanity.

Romero does not agree with those who hold that there is a clear line of demarcation between culture and nature, i.e., that culture is produced by man, and nature is independent of him. If man is an animal—as some would claim—his creations are just as natural as those of lower forms of animal life. Or conversely, a bird's nest is as much a cultural product, the result of purposeful activity as an architect's building.

No, the distinction is not so much between nature and culture, as it is between nature and spirit. Man is both nature and spirit. Within man the natural may predominate or it may develop into spiritual attitudes. Of course, he is never pure spirit. If, as Romero has been saying all along, man is characterized by intentional activity (which produces culture), and this intentionality can be spiritualized, then "nature," within this framework, is equivalent to non-spiritualized intentionality.[73]

The characteristic note of man is to perceive objects. He possesses intentional, objective consciousness. This makes it possible for him to operate within a world of objects in contrast to the animal which has only a "state of consciousness." Man's ability to confront objects, his "objectifying faculty."[74] makes possible the existence of a human community, and this, chiefly through the medium of language.[75] Language plus intentionality enable man to capture his environment of objects, as well as to look upon himself as an object. If the individual is an intentional being, then the human community as a whole can be said to be an "intentional community."[76] The human or intentional community produces culture. In order to act upon one's environment, it is necessary to objectify it. An object which is the result of an intentional activity is a cultural product.

A possible difficulty may be said to emerge at this point, one related once again to a definition of terms. It is true that man creates culture as a result of his intentional psy-

chism; he "culturizes" nature. He is capable of "objectivizing," of which the last and highest step in the process is
"transcending" or "spiritualizing" the relationship between
the self and the object. But what actually, one may ask,
is "intentionality?" According to Romero, this is what
distinguishes man from animal. Yet as Risieri Frondizi
points out,[77] Romero himself admits that a vague suggestion
of intentionality may possibly exist even in some animals. If
this is so, then the distinction between man and animal is no
longer so hard and fast. Intentionality is no longer the exclusive monopoly of man.

Moreover, asks Frondizi, where does intentionality end
and spirituality begin? Is the latter a *continuation* of the
former or are they two separate entities? Does the first flow
into the second, or is there a break between the two? Similarly, in connection with Romero's conception of different
levels of reality whereby each successive level rests upon a
lower form, the question may well be asked: Is the realm of
the spirit an extension, a continuation, of the world of
nature, or is there a deep gulf which separates the two?

Man is an historical reality within which "mere intentionality and spirit alternate and are joined together."[78]
Man's duality has long been recognized in religious as well
as philosophic thought. For example, the idea of salvation
implies the existence of this duality: man has to be re-
deemed from his natural state and given the possibility of
achieving perfection in a superior order. The opposition
between the vital and the spiritual is another illustration of
duality. The vital, i.e., spontaneous life, represents intentionality, competition and conflict. The spirit, as we have
seen, is equivalent to harmony and universality. However,
given the human condition of man, it is impossible to conceive of a community dominated by the purely spiritual. The
very basis of man's existence is intentional. Denying this
intentionality would be tantamount to annihilating the
spirit, since the latter thrives on the presence of the
former. The spirit must subdue and control mere inten-

tionality; it must organize it in harmonious fashion in accordance with acceptable standards.

The youthful adolescent suffers keenly from the clash of this duality. On the one hand, mere intentionality, overpowering in its demands, has not yet been brought under control by social pressures. On the other, the spiritual values, deeply experienced, are not realized effectively in the business of daily living.[79]

As one achieves a relative degree of maturity, a sort of uneasy truce is arrived at; a more or less stable equilibrium is reached in which each human being works out his own formula for resolving the conflict between the intentional and spiritual components. The formula must serve not only to insure one's own internal balance, i.e., one's inner peace of mind, but also an equilibrium which involves a relatively satisfactory, external relationship, i.e., between the individual and his environment.[80] The relations between man and institutions, give rise to constant attempts to preserve, modify and/or reform and replace. Both innovation and resistance to change take place in all cultural domains and, as a result, generate tensions within individuals. The educational process represents an effort to resolve these tensions by attempting to raise human beings to the desired average cultural level.

✓   ✓   ✓

Duality, referred to above, gives rise to "masking." Animals, unlike man, never feel that they have to justify their actions. By contrast, man disguises his relationship with others as well as with himself in a number of different ways.[81] This is what Romero refers to as "wearing a mask." What is masked or disguised remains intact. The masking process may be performed consciously or unconsciously. In either case, the subject is convinced that what is hidden deserves to be, since his self needs to be assured of its self-respect. Masking will therefore take place in order to repress certain intentional acts which may not be in harmony with the image one has of oneself and wishes to perpetuate, or in accord with certain principles and standards adhered to by the subject—the result of community pressures and traditions. This masking process is not necessarily dictated by the spiritual principle. It takes place also on the lower, merely intentional level for reasons of personal prestige.

Masking assumes various degrees of subtlety. On the lowest organic level, for example, biological appetites may be disguised. A more subtle example would involve self-justification, i.e., masking the motives of one's acts in order to avoid detracting from one's dignity; in short, a defense mechanism utilized to present a favorable impression to oneself. For purposes of illustration, Romero refers to Scheler's discussion of the phenomenon of resentment. Man negates, downgrades or deceives himself with respect to those values which he cannot attain, in order to escape the feeling of inferiority engendered by resentment at not being able to live according to these values. Or else, these values are replaced by the illusion, at least, of other values which serve to relieve the tension caused by resentment. Self-justification, then, serves to mask motives. In phenomena of resentment it is generally the practice "to criticize a person severely and if possible even to inflict harm upon him while believing sincerely that a sense of strict justice is being observed, whereas in reality it is resentment that governs these acts."[82]

Man does not utilize the mechanism of self-deception only in the case of individual acts. He may also do so with respect to the course of his entire life. For is it not true that one's autobiography, written in the twilight of one's existence, often stems from the need to justify oneself? True, this purpose may not have motivated the book originally; nevertheless instances of self-justification tend to crop up continually as one thumbs the pages.

Romero's discussion concerning the masking process points to the rather disconcerting conclusion that the problem of self-knowledge is apparently insoluble. It is impossible to really "know thyself." Knowledge of what is external, i.e., that which comes via the senses, "is not manifested as it is in reality."[83] By contrast, what is perceived within one's inner reality "does not suffer from the distortion of sensory instruments."[84] Yet it has already been suggested that the authenticity of self-perception and apprehension of inner reality tends to suffer from masking and self-deceptive interpretations. Self-knowledge, then, is fraught with difficulties and contradictions. An introspective person, for example, in contrast to the extrovert, tends to avoid many circumstances, or else he selects others more in keeping with his personality within which he is prepared to function. Yet by this very act, the reflective introvert offers us fewer opportunities to see what he is really like. Not only does he not reveal himself to others; he conceals his personality from himself and thereby renders self-knowledge impossible. And Romero concludes:

> "True knowledge of oneself can be attained only by a means of balanced integration of self-perception, one's own retrospective vision of oneself, the acceptance of our image which is formed by others, and an external, posterior, panoramic inspection which would record all the articulations of the self as concerns that which is prior and coetaneous with it, and which would therefore be capable of giving an account of all questions dealing with origins and interconnections."[85]

Of course, the masking process would have to be eliminated completely. Since such a prospect would seem quite unlikely, we would have to be content with partialities, fragments and variables. Complete integration is impossible.

Man as a dual entity not only develops in response to both individual and group motivations, but is also capable of acceding to and acting upon demands which are paramount in the shaping of an ideal order. In short, man is capable of responding to rarer instances of spiritualized intentionality as well as to what is more usual, namely, mere intentionality. Historical man is, thus, a mixture, "a complex in which mere intentionality and spirit alternate and are joined together."[86] Man functions as a subject, confronting an objective order to be acted upon. He is not closed off from the world. On the contrary, he "opens himself to the world;

152

he is not an organism that is limited to receiving or avoiding impacts . . ."[87] Yet he not only goes out toward the world; he also brings the world to himself. "Self" and "world" are in constant juxtaposition, in a continual dynamic interrelationship. Self cannot exist without world; world without self is also an empty possibility. For just as the self tends toward objectivities, the world needs the self in order to be known and to be utilized intelligently.

In dealing with ethical values, Romero establishes certain categories in relation to the self or the "I." The categories so established vary within themselves in meaning and import, depending upon whether a merely intentional or a spiritual attitude happens to be dominant.

For example, in contradistinction to "self," one's neighbor as seen by that self, is designated as the "other." Frequently this "other" may be referred to as a "thou." In that case a personal relationship is implied. Each of the "others" is a "he;" "they" and "others" are therefore identical.

The term "we" now presents interesting possibilities. Romero makes a telling point in this connection: ". . . every 'thou' implies a 'we' for the 'I,' but the 'I,' does not consider as 'thou's' all those who comprise together with him the different kinds of 'we'."[88]

From the standpoint of mere intentionality, characterized by the so-called "subjective return," the "we's" are merely amplifications of the "I" or the self. It is possible at times for the "I" to rise above mere intentionality and sacrifice himself in "disinterested" fashion for the good of the "we," and yet the "we" or the group may well continue to stress its own collective egotistical interests. In this case, the "I" evinces a spiritual attitude (in its intentions) or in other words, an absolute value, in spite of the fact that the group does not operate on that level at all.

On the other hand, if the "we" assumes a spiritual position similar to that of the "I," then the group behavior in question also lacks the subjective return, i.e., the "we" does not benefit from its acts. Romero thus distinguishes between two types of "we's." The merely intentional "we" is interested only in its own needs, gains and purposes; the spiritual "we" is interested only in giving, not in appropriating.

And yet, even if one were to operate within the strict framework of the merely intentional "we," one would tend to approach the realm of spiritualization, simply because the very existence of "we" and the human contact which this implies, lead one directly to a "thou." The "thou," in turn, stimulates the awareness of a "him" and by that time, one may well be on the way to engaging in a spiritual experience. In order to achieve an authentically absolute, ethical attitude, the self must consider itself as well as the "thou" as divorced from the merely intentional motivations, which means viewing the "I" and the "thou" as a "him," and accepting this "him" or this "other" not as a thing, but as a self.

Romero distinguishes between what he calls "sociability" and ethical behavior. Sociability precedes ethical behavior. Sociability, in the process of human relations, involves an element of subjective return. "Any special connection between the subject of the act and an 'other' gives rise to a 'thou,' who for the subject of the act is 'his thou,' and an 'I' that calls forth a particular interest because it is somehow 'his'. . ." (i.e., the subject's).[89] In contrast, transcendence or ethical value occurs when "an 'I' is not related to one's own self in any particular concrete way . . . when we treat our own 'I' as we would a 'him'."[90]

Every "thou" opens up the possibility of possession from the viewpoint of the "I," e.g., my brother, my friend. This is a connection denied to the others. The "I-thou" relationship lends itself more readily to the "subjective return," since the factor of intentionality with respect to the "thou" as an object is present in the consciousness of the "I." In order for the "I" to transcend the egotistical sphere, with relation to the "thou," it would help if the "thou" were to lose its "thou-ness," i.e., to eliminate the "I-thou" alliance, which can be of benefit to "I."

The purely ethical relationship, then, is established with

the "him," not with the "thou," because the "I" has the feeling that somehow the "thou," belongs to him, which makes it more likely to expect a subjective return. It would seem, therefore, that the "thou" would have to lose its "thou-ness" and become a "he," in order for a properly ethical quality to be assumed by the "I."

From all of the above, we derive the fact that the human self cannot exist in isolation. If the intentional self needs the "thou's" and the "we's," the spiritual self cannot do without the "they's" in order to permeate and work its will throughout the whole of humanity.

The "I-thou" should be a bridge, leading to the "I-he," for "he," i.e., one's fellow-man, is an "almost-thou." At times, "he" is an "almost-thing." But "he" should be much more than just a thing. "He" has an "I" of his own. It is easier to perceive the "I" in a "thou," than in a distant "he." Romero therefore seems to imply that it is more difficult for "I" to act "disinterestedly" in the case of "he." In order, then, to achieve the highest spiritual level, it is necessary to place the emphasis, not upon the "I" or the "thou," but upon the "he."

In short, changing the "other" to a "thou" implies the emergence of a relative ethical value, because of the subjective interest involved. On the other hand, changing the "other," the "thou" or the "I" to a "him" is a prerequisite for achieving an absolute ethical value.

Once again in this respect, Romero speaks of the distinction between intention and end result. An act is defined as ethical in the light of its intention, not its result or achievement. If the act is transcendent in its intention, it possesses ethical value even though it does not succeed in the purpose for which it was originally conceived. Conversely, the act will not be considered ethical if transcendence is lacking in the intention, even if the result of that act seems to bear the imprint of ethical activity. There are, then, ethical acts and ethical objectifications. The latter, e.g., norms and institutions, depend on and are judged by their efficiency, i.e., by the degree of adequacy with which they have satisfied their purpose and meaning. If objectification "does not serve ethical purposes, it does not transcend itself and remains immanent within itself."[91]

Romero's formulation would seem to resolve the conflict in ethical doctrine between those who assert that there are no duties except those toward others, and those who maintain that there are obligations only toward oneself. Romero synthesizes the two points of view. Duty toward oneself is the equivalent of duty toward an "I:" not an "I" which is "my I," but rather an "I" which is considered as a "he." This "he," in turn, is respected as an "I," whose very essence it is to project itself toward the other.

*   *   *

Man can conceive of two different worlds; that which is and that which ought to be. This is essentially what can be referred to as the "human condition:" positing the premise that something ought to exist even though it may never have a chance to materialize. As a consequence, man goes on forging, creating, building and modifying ideas, norms, customs and institutions; in this way he realizes himself as man and makes it possible for his descendants to do likewise.[92]

In this world of culture, painfully erected by man, and whose account is related by history, the role of philosophy becomes evident. Philosophy is the consciousness of culture, culture turned inward upon itself and meditating upon itself. For just as there is no man who is not conscious of himself, so similarly is it impossible to conceive of culture without humanity's taking stock of itself and evaluating its achievements. This is the task of philosophy. In fact, without culture there can be no humanity, just as man without culture would be reduced to the level of the beast or that of an automaton. Philosophy emerges precisely at the point at which culture becomes a problem or an idea which bears discussion and which seeks solutions.[93]

History can be described as the process of man's humanization, i.e., his realization, or the development of what he was meant to be. In the words of Herder, the goal of history is humanity. That which is typically human is the spirit which seeks without rest that which *ought* to be. History, then, is a steady progression from nature toward spirit; history strives to subdue and control blind nature, and replace it with the role of the spiritual principle. Since nature is necessity and fatality, and spirit represents freedom, then history is the gradual conquest of freedom; it represents the struggle against the oppressive forces of blind nature both outside and within man himself. And what is it that must be vanquished? Ignorance, violence, and egotism.[94] If philosophy is the inner conscience of culture, it becomes obvious that it cannot be separated from freedom. The latter is the *sine qua non* for research and investigation; without it, there can be no philosophy. The search for truth has a long and distinguished history. Ever since the early days of classical antiquity, philosophy has tried to triumph over ignorance and appearance.

Every critical period is a period of confusion during which time explanations are urgently demanded. It is a near certainty that the present crisis is related to a renewed interest in philosophy. In reciprocal fashion, philosophy is faced with the urgent task of having to re-examine, re-think and re-evaluate the various segments of the culture of which it is itself a component part. In this respect—and here we have a repetition of the basic theme—philosophy will have to illuminate the way for man to increase his spiritual potential and thus advance along the path toward the realization of himself as more of a person than he is at present.[95]

It was precisely because he was a philosopher, that Romero was most interested in the preservation and extension of man's freedom. Freedom, he maintained, cannot be parcelled out and divided into separate compartments, so that it may be said to exist in some but not in others. To say that one can be free to investigate the sciences or to cultivate the arts in an atmosphere characterized by the suppression of political liberties, would be an untenable position. The most basic and generalized form of freedom is political in nature. Without assurance of political freedom, any degree of permissiveness in science, art or philosophy, is contingent. Political freedom is the indispensable guarantee for all other freedoms.

It is perhaps the realm of philosophy which suffers most when liberties are suppressed. Philosophy and freedom are inseparable.[96] Dictators, for example, fear independent thinking. The dictatorial mentality believes itself possessed of all truth. Faced by this type of situation, the philosopher who expresses the truth as he understands it, is forced either to accept the dictator's truth, in which case he surrenders his claim to authentic philosophy or else, he becomes an exile if he chooses to continue as a philosopher, or ceases to philosophize if he is to remain in his country. Political freedom is not a charitable gift bestowed by governmental authorities, but rather a right, to be exercised with dignity.

Romero, like Korn, may well be called "the philosopher of freedom." This is an especially fitting description in view of the political climate in which he found himself. In 1930, following a period of political unrest, a military coup brought General Uriburu into power. His regime was markedly influenced by Fascist ideology of the Mussolini variety. The scepticism and disillusionment of the great mass of Argentines was matched by governing procedures that can only be described as "fraudulent democracy."[97] With the outbreak of World War II, the ruling clique showed open sympathy for the Axis Powers, although public opinion was certainly not favorably disposed toward Hitler's Germany. The culminating point in the trajectory was reached when Juan Perón gained control of the government. Thus, Francisco Romero was destined to experience a quarter of a century of Argentine fascism.

Romero's attitude in these circumstances is well synthesized in the following assertion:

> Authoritarianism of the totalitarian type has already given abundant evidence, in all countries where it has imposed itself, of its efficacy in the destruction of spiritual values; and of all these values, that which is con-

cerned with the search for truth is one of the most vulnerable.[98]

Romero did not only teach philosophy; he *lived* it. In, 1942, as a member of the *Colegio Libre de Estudios Superiores,* he signed a petition, addressed to Congress, requesting that the state of sicge be lifted. In 1946, during the Perón regime, he resigned from the Universities of Buenos Aires and La Plata, as a protest against the decision of the government to intervene in the direction of institutions of higher learning.

His consistent and courageous linking of theory with action resulted not only in economic hardship, but also in imprisonment—an event which called forth vigorous condemnation on the part of distinguished personalities in various countries. The conspiracy of silence with which the dictatorship sought to cloak his activities, in a vain attempt at concealing its own vulnerability, proved to no avail. Ironically enough, it was only when political conditions forced him to curtail his teaching activities, that he was able to devote more time to writing and, as a result, bring forth his *Theory of Man.*

The close alliance between philosophy and liberty is based on the fact that philosophy is at least in part the theoretical expression of freedom. It is the self-awareness of a culture, and culture is composed of the endless series of efforts on the part of man to achieve freedom. Man, according to Romero's predecessor and teacher, Alejandro Korn, endeavors to attain a greater measure of freedom in the course of his struggle against nature, as a result of clash and strife with his fellow-man, and finally, as an outgrowth of his continual conflict with himself. His goals are therefore: control of nature, adequate and healthy social organization, and personal self-sufficiency.*

In this process of culture formation and realization, philosophy has always played the role of liberating man from external as well as internal obstacles in order to enable

---
* See Chapter 3.

159

him to achieve the full measure of human dignity. The philosophy of history teaches us that ever since the abandonment of theological and providential interpretations of man's behavior, "history is revealed as a laborious process of liberation."[99] At this point, Romero once again resorts to his basic structure, outlined in his philosophical anthropology. Freedom is identified with spirit, and spirit is the higher element residing in man which gives rise to and develops culture. Even when man chooses not to act "spiritually," but merely "intentionally," with reference to his individual or group needs and interests, he exercises some measure of freedom, in that he transcends blind, pre-destined animal instincts. His freedom is even greater when he acts "spiritually," for then he has transcended his own interests as a particular individual and now acts in accordance with universal norms and values, in short as a "person."[100]

No culture, worthy of the name, is conceivable without philosophy. For man, unlike animal, has two worlds: that which he is and partakes of, and that which he ought to be. This latter world causes man to exert himself, to create, to realize to the optimum degree the plenitude of his being, and to make it possible for his descendants to do likewise in even greater measure. In this process of making history, philosophy has its role to play, its task to fulfil, namely, that of evaluating continually. Just as it is impossible for man to exist without a corresponding self-awareness, it is similarly inconceivable for a culture to go on functioning without its taking stock of itself, without judging and evaluating.[101] Culture matures and constitutes the material for problem solving—the task of philosophy—at the same time that man becomes increasingly humanized.

✼ ✼ ✼

Romero was an indefatigable worker. Not only did he dedicate himself completely to university teaching; he also edited works in European philosophy, directed numerous publications, and maintained a vast correspondence. He conceived his mission to be that of leading the entire Latin

American continent along the road to philosophic matura-
tion. So time-consuming was this grandiose project of his,
that it left him little time for original, creative writing. An
indispensable pre-requisite for the realization of his mission
was the unfettered exercise of freedom. In fact, for Romero, the American experience *per se* is the very essence of
freedom: freedom from economic, religious and political
oppression, freedom to open up the widest horizons in
order to assimilate universal values to the American scene.[102]
American historical reality—that of a continent in evolution
—implies a refusal to abide by provincial limitations. The
American idea is analogous to sympathy for and compre-
hension of everything that is human; it is a synonym for
freedom to accept or reject, adopt and modify. It is at this
point that freedom and universality merge.

The philosophy of Romero can perhaps be said to be a
refreshing contrast to the all-pervading anguish, melancholy
and overpowering sense of absurdity and desolation, so
characteristic of certain sectors on the contemporary scene.
It is essentially expansive and optimistic. One might well
say it is extrovert in that its whole direction is an outward
projection toward the realization and conquest of ever-
broadening and far-reaching horizons.

There have always been two types of philosophers, just
as there have always been two types of artists: those who
are content to observe and interpret reality, and those who
endeavor to transform it. Romero belongs to the second
category. The philosopher, he believed, should not write
only for the specialist, but for the *man;* he should emerge
from his ivory tower and *humanize* what he has to say.

Romero was not only an activist; he was also an optimist.
Or perhaps he was so active, precisely *because* he was dominated by a creative optimism—and this at a time when
his native land seemed saturated with intense pessimism.
Shortly before his death, he wrote that it was necessary to
conquer the "absurd pessimism" of the moment, and "to
strengthen the creative energies." And further: "I have

infinite faith in man ... all life, especially the spiritual aspect, is overflowing, generous, creative and self-giving."*

Well may these last words serve to illustrate the quintessence of this philosopher and above all, the person. Well may they also highlight the trajectory that illuminates that portion of the philosophic canvas of Argentina, which begins with José Ingenieros and ends with Francisco Romero.

---

* In a letter to a friend, dated February 26, 1962.

Selected Bibliography

Agosti, Hector P., *José Ingenieros, ciudadano de la juventud*. Buenos Aires, 1945.

Alvárez Forn, Raúl, "La idea de cultura en la filosofía de Francisco Romero," *Ciudad*. Buenos Aires, 4-5, 1956, pp. 43-48.

Ameghino, Florentino, "Mi credo," *Obras completas*. La Plata, 1934.

Bagú, Sergio, *La vida ejemplar de José Ingenieros*. Buenos Aires, 1936.

Barja, César, "Alejandro Korn," *Revista iberoamericana*. Vol. II, no. 4, noviembre de 1940, pp. 359-382.

Barreda Laos, Felipe, *Vida intelectual de la colonia*. Lima, 1909.

Bermann, Gregorio, "La filosofía de Ingenieros," *Revista de Filosofía*. (Buenos Aires) XII, No. 1, pp. 178-231.

Blanco Fambona, Rufino, *Grandes escritores de América*, Madrid, 1917.

Brightman, Edgar S., "Structure and Transcendence of the Thought of Francisco Romero," *Philosophy and Phenomenological Research*. Buffalo, December 1943, pp. 133-141.

Bunge, Carlos O., *Estudios filosóficos*. Buenos Aires, 1919.

Caturelli, Alberto, *La filosofía en Argentina actual*. Córdoba, 1962.

Comte, Auguste, *Discourse of Positivist Philosophy*. Paris, 1844.

————, *System of Positivist Politics*. Paris, 1852-1854.

Crawford, William R., *A Century of Latin American Thought*. Cambridge, 1944.

Diffie, Bailey W., *Latin American Civilization*. Harrisburg, 1945.

Dujovne, León, *La obra filosófica de José Ingenieros*. Buenos Aires, 1930.

Endara, Julio, *José Ingenieros y el porvenir de la filosofía*. Buenos Aires, 1921.

Farré, Luis, *Cincuenta años de filosofía en Argentina*. Buenos Aires, 1958.

Fránquiz, José A., "El estructuralismo personalista del profesor Francisco Romero," *Luminar*. México, IV, No. 2, 1940, pp. 252-275.

Frondizi, Risieri, "Hay una filosofía iberoamericana?" *Realidad, Revista de ideas*. Buenos Aires, III, 8, marzo-abril de 1948, pp. 158-170.

————, "La teoría del hombre de Francisco Romero," *Filosofía y letras*. México, Vol. XXV, No. 49-50, enero-junio de 1953.

Galíndez, Jorge, "Korn, filósofo de la libertad," *Cursos y conferencias*. Buenos Aires, octubre-noviembre de 1946, pp. 31-35.

González, Julio V., *La emancipación de la universidad*. Buenos Aires, 1929.

Harris, Marjorie, *Francisco Romero on Problems of Philosophy*. New York, Philosophical Library, 1960.

Herring, Hubert, *A History of Latin America*. New York, Appleton-Century, 1961.

Homenaje a Francisco Romero. University of Buenos Aires, 1964.

Hussey, Roland D., "Traces of French Enlightenment in Colonial Hispanic America," Whitaker, Arthur P., *Latin America and the Enlightenment*. New York, Appleton-Century, 1942.

Ingenieros, José, *El hombre mediocre*. Buenos Aires, 1917.

————, *Emilio Boutroux y la filosofía universitaria en Francia*. Buenos Aires, 1923.

————, *Hacia una moral sin dogmas: lecciones sobre el eticismo*. Buenos Aires, 1919.

————, *La cultura filosófica en España*. Madrid (?) 1916.

————, *La evolución de las ideas argentinas*. Buenos Aires, 1918-1920.

————, *Las doctrinas de Ameghino: la tierra, la vida y el hombre*. Buenos Aires, 1919.

————, *La fuerzas morales*. Buenos Aires, 1926.

————, *Le Dantec, biólogo y filósofo*. Buenos Aires, 1928.

————, *Los tiempos nuevos*. Buenos Aires, 1921.

————, *Principios de psicología biológica*. Madrid, 1913.

————, *Proposiciones relativas al porvenir de la filosofía*. Buenos Aires, 1918.

Insúa Rodríguez, Ramón, *Historia de la filosofía hispanoamericana.* Guayaquil, 1945.

Kilgore, William J., "Alejandro Korn y la teoría relativista de los valores," *Philosophia.* Mendoza, No. 23, 1959.

—————, "Estudios sobre Alejandro Korn," *Homenaje en el centenario de su nacimiento.* La Plata, agosto de 1963.

Korn, Alejandro, *Obras completas.* Buenos Aires, 1949.

Lanning, John R., *Academic Culture in the Spanish Colonies.* New York, Oxford University Press, 1940.

—————, "The Reception of the Enlightenment," Whitaker, Arthur P., *Latin America and the Enlightenment.* New York, Appleton-Century, 1942.

Mannheim, Karl, *Ideology and Utopia.* New York, Harcourt, Brace and Co., 1946.

Massuh, Víctor, "Cultura de oriente y crisis occidental según Francisco Romero," *Ciudad.* Buenos Aires, 4-5, 1956, pp. 49-53.

Méndez Bejarano, Mario, *Historia de la filosofía en España hasta el siglo XX.* Madrid, 192—.

Mercante, Víctor, "La obra moral de Ingenieros," *Revista de Filosofía.* Buenos Aires, XII, No. 1, enero de 1926, pp. 140-177.

de Onís, Federico, *Ensayos sobre el sentido de la cultura española.* Madrid, 1932.

Orgaz, Raúl A., "Ingenieros, sociólogo," *Revista de Filosofía.* Buenos Aires, XII, No. 1, enero de 1926, pp. 96-113.

Perelstein, Berta, *Positivismo y anti-positivismo en la Argentina.* Buenos Aires, 1952.

Piérola, Raúl A., "Alejandro Korn y el pensamiento contemporáneo," *Cursos y conferencias.* Buenos Aires, octubre-noviembre de 1946, pp. 7-20.

Ponce, Aníbal, "Para una historia de Ingenieros," *Revista de Filosofía,* Buenos Aires, XII, No. 1, enero de 1926, pp. 1-82.

Primer Congreso de Filosofía y Filosofía de la Educación, Quito, 1954.

Pucciarelli, Eugenio, "Alejandro Korn y el pensamiento europeo," *Revista de la Universidad Nacional de La Plata.* La Plata, No. 12, septiembre-diciembre de 1960, pp. 29-55.

—————, "Alejandro Korn, maestro de saber y de virtud," *Cursos y conferencias.* Buenos Aires, enero de 1937, pp. 1067-1086.

Rodríguez-Alcalá, Hugo, *Misión y pensamiento de Francisco Romero*. México, 1959.

Rodríguez Bustamante, Norberto, "Los apuntes filosóficos de Korn," *Cursos y conferencias*. Buenos Aires, octubre-noviembre de 1946, pp. 21-24.

————, "Persona y libertad en la filosofía de Francisco Romero," *Ciudad*, Buenos Aires, 4-5, 1956, pp. 36-42.

Romero, Francisco, *Alejandro Korn, filósofo de la libertad*. Buenos Aires, 1956.

————, "Diagnóstico y pronóstico de al crisis," *Imago Mundi*. Buenos Aires, III, No. 11-12, marzo-junio de 1956, pp. 33-41.

————, *El hombre y la cultura*. Buenos Aires, 1956.

————, *Estudios de historia de las ideas*. Buenos Aires, 1953.

————, *Filosofía contemporánea*. Buenos Aires, 1953.

————, *Filosofía de ayer y de hoy*. Madrid, 1960.

————, *Filosofía de la persona*. Buenos Aires, 1944.

————, "Filosofía y libertad," *Asociación argentina por la libertad de la cultura*. Buenos Aires, 1956.

————, *Filósofos y problemas*. Buenos Aires, 1947.

————, *Ideas y figuras*. Buenos Aires, 1949.

————, "Las alianzas de la filosofía," *La Torre*, Universidad de Puerto Rico, año II, núm. 6, junio de 1954.

————, *Papeles para una filosofía*. Buenos Aires, 1945.

————, *Programa de una filosofía*. Buenos Aires, 1940.

————, *Relaciones de la filosofía*. Buenos Aires, 1958.

————, *Sobre la filosofía en América*. Buenos Aires, 1952.

————, *Teoría del hombre*. Buenos Aires, 1952. (English translation: *Theory of Man*, by William F. Cooper, University of California Press, 1964.)

Romero, Francisco, Vasallo, Angel and Aznar, Luis Z., *Alejandro Korn*. Buenos Aires, 1940.

Romero, José L., *Argentina: imágenes y perspectivas*. Buenos Aires, 1956.

————, *Las ideas políticas en Argentina*. Buenos Aires, 1946.

Salazar Bondy, Augusto, "Notas sobre las ideas axiológicas de Francisco Romero," *Homenaje a Francisco Romero*. Universidad de Buenos Aires, 1964.

Sánchez Reulet, Aníbal, "Alejandro Korn," *Sur*. Buenos Aires, enero de 1937, pp. 87-92.

Scheler, Max, *Die Wissensformen und die Gesellschaft*. Leipzig, 1926.

Soler, Ricaurte, *El positivismo argentino*. Panamá, 1959.

Sierra Mejía, Rubén, "Francisco Romero," *Ideas y valores*. Bogotá, Vol. IV, no. 15-16, octubre de 1962—marzo de 1963, pp. 71-75.

Torchia-Estrada, Juan C., "La concepción antropológica de Francisco Romero," *Ciudad*. Buenos Aires, 4-5, 1956, pp. 21-29.

————, *La Filosofía en la Argentina*. Washington, D.C., 1961.

Vitier, Medardo, "La filosofía de don Alejandro Korn," *Revista cubana*. La Habana, julio-diciembre de 1940, pp. 133-142.

Whitaker, Arthur P., *Latin America and the Enlightenment*. New York, Appleton-Century Co., 1942.

Wilson, Irma, *Mexico: A Century of educational thought*. New York, Hispanic Institute in the United States of America, 1941.

Zea, Leopoldo, *Apogeo y decadencia del positivismo en México*. México, 1944.

————, *Dos etapas del pensamiento en Hispanoamérica: del romanticismo al positivismo*. México, 1949.

Zum Felde, Alberto, *El problema de la cultura americana*. Buenos Aires, 1943.

References

CHAPTER ONE

1. Ramón Insúa Rodríguez, *Historia de la filosofía hispanoamericana,* Guayaquil, 1945, p. 41.
2. Ibid., p. 42.
3. Alberto Zum Felde, *El Problema de la cultura americana,* Buenos Aires, 1943, p. 197.
4. Ibid., p. 194.
5. Federico de Onís, *Ensayos sobre el sentido de la cultura española,* Madrid, 1932, p. 100. Mario Méndez Bejarano, *Historia de la filosofía en España hasta el siglo xx,* Madrid, 192—, p. 342.
6. Julio V. González, *La Emancipación de la universidad,* Buenos Aires, 1929, p. 5
7. Bailey W. Diffie, *Latin American Civilization,* Harrisburg, 1945, p. 545.
8. Insúa Rodríguez, op. cit., p. 104.
9. John T. Lanning: "The Reception of the Enlightenment in Latin America," in Arthur P. Whitaker, *Latin America and the Enlightenment,* New York, 1942, p. 75.
10. Diffie, op. cit., p. 547, footnote no. 11.
11. John T. Lanning, *Academic Culture in the Spanish Colonies,* New York, 1940, p. 66.
12. Ibid., pp. 68-69.
13. Ibid., p. 68.
14. Ibid., p. 69.
15. Roland D. Hussay, "Traces of French Enlightenment in Colonial Hispanic America," in Whitaker, op. cit., p. 29.
16. Lanning, *Academic Culture,* p. 70.
17. Diffie, op. cit., p. 142.
18. John A. Mackay, *The Other Spanish Christ,* New York, 1933, p. 63.
19. Lanning, *Academic Culture.* p. 89.
20. Irma Wilson, *Mexico: A Century of Educational Thought,* New York, 1941, p. 53.
21. Felipe Barreda Laos, *Vida intelectual de la colonia,* Lima, 1909, p. 395.
22. Juan Carlos Torchia-Estrada, *La Filosofía en la Argentina,* Washington, D.C., 1961, p. 79, pp. 88-89.
23. José Luis Romero, *Argentina: Imágenes y perspectivas,* Buenos Aires, 1956, p. 25.
24. Alejandro Korn, *Obras completas,* Buenos Aires, 1949, p. 135.

25. Leopoldo Zea, *Dos etapas del pensamiento en Hispanoamérica: del romanticismo al positivismo*, México, 1949, p. 42.
26. Korn, op. cit., p. 30.
27. Torchia-Estrada, op. cit., p. 123.
28. *Primer Congreso de Filosofía y Filosofía de la Educación*, Quito, 1954, p. 186.
29. Ricaurte Soler, *El Positivismo argentino*, Panamá, 1959, p. 51.
30. Ibid., pp. 57-58.
31. Berta Perelstein, *Positivismo y anti-positivismo en la Argentina*, Buenos Aires, 1952.
32. Auguste Comte, *Discourse of Positivist Philosophy*, Paris, 1844, Lesson 4.
33. Auguste Comte, *System of Positivist Politics*, Paris, 1852-1854.
34. Insúa Rodríguez, op. cit., p. 186.
34a. Risieri Frondizi, "Hay una filosofía iberoamericana?" *Realidad, Revista de ideas*, Buenos Aires, marzo-abril de 1948, p. 163.
35. loc cit.
36. Zea, op. cit., p. 43 ff.
37. Leopoldo Zea, *Apogeo y Decadencia del positivismo en México*, México, 1944, p. 213.
38. Karl Mannheim, *Ideology and Utopia*, New York, 1946, pp. 73-74.
38a. Zea, *Dos etapas*, pp. 279-280.
39. José Luis Romero, *Las ideas políticas en Argentina*, Buenos Aires, 1946, p. 186.
40. Zea, *Dos etapas*, p. 293.
41. Max Scheler, *Die Wissensformen und die Gesellschaft*, Leipzig, 1926, p. 207.
42. Francisco Romero, *Sobre la filosofía en América*, Buenos Aires, 1952, p. 23.
43. Korn, op. cit., p. 150.
44. Torchia-Estrada, op. cit., p. 129.
45. Korn, op. cit., p. 150.
46. Torchia-Estrada, op. cit. p. 173.
47. José Ingenieros, *Las doctrinas de Ameghino*, Buenos Aires, 1919, p. 212.
48. Florentino Ameghino, "Mi credo," *Obras completas*, La Plata, 1934, vol. 15, p. 691.
49. loc. cit.
50. José Luis Romero, *Las ideas políticas*, p. 167.
51. Hubert Herring, *A History of Latin America*, New York, 1961, p. 657.
52. Korn, op. cit., p. 173.
52a. Farré, Luis,, *Cincuenta años de filosofía en Argentina*, Buenos Aires, 1958, p. 59.
53. Carlos Octavio Bunge, *Estudios filosóficos*, Buenos Aires, 1919, p. 46.
54. op. cit., pp. 8-9. (Introduction by Enrique Martínez Paz).
55. Perelstein, op. cit., p. 143.

CHAPTER TWO

1. Francisco Romero, *Sobre la filosofía en América*, Buenos Aires, 1952, p. 34.

1a. José Luis Romero, *Las ideas políticas en Argentina*, Buenos Aires, 1946, p. 186.
1b. Héctor P. Agosti, *José Ingenieros*, Buenos Aires, 1945, p. 17.
1c. Aníbal Ponce, "Para una historia de Ingenieros," *Revista de filosofía*, Buenos Aires, vol. XII, núm. 1, enero de 1926, p. 6.
1d. op. cit., p. 8.
2. José Ingenieros, *Principios de psicología biológica*, Madrid, 1913, p. 437.
3. op. cit., p. 331.
4. Soler, op. cit., p. 103.
5. León Dujovne, *La obra filosófica de José Ingenieros*, Buenos Aires, 1930, p. 26.
6. Ingenieros, op. cit., p. 112.
7. Torchia-Estrada, op. cit., p. 214.
8. Ingenieros, op. cit., p. 140.
9. Dujovne, op. cit., p. 34.
10. Ingenieros, op. cit., p. 234, p. 283 ff.
11. op. cit., p. 265 ff.
12. op. cit., pp. 358-359.
13. op. cit., p. 30
14. op. cit., p. 35 ff.
15. op. cit., p. 45.
16. José Ingenieros, *Proposiciones relativas al porvenir de la filosofía*, Buenos Aires, 1957, p. 13.
17. op. cit., p. 15.
18. op. cit., pp. 16-17.
19. op. cit., pp. 17-18.
20. Francisco Romero, op. cit., p. 37.
21. Ingenieros, *Proposiciones*, p. 22, footnote 4.
22. op. cit., p. 32.
23. loc. cit.
24. op. cit., p. 33.
25. op. cit., p. 37.
26. op. cit., p. 36.
27. op. cit., p. 37.
28. op. cit., p. 38.
29. op. cit., p. 39.
30. op. cit., p. 40, footnote.
31. op. cit., p. 44.
32. loc. cit.
33. Gregorio Bermann, "La Filosofía de Ingenieros," *Revista de Filosofía*, op. cit., p. 201.
34. Ingenieros, *Proposiciones*, p. 32.
35. op. cit., p. 33.
36. op. cit., p. 46.
37. op. cit., p. 32.
38. op. cit., p. 56.
39. op. cit., p. 63 ff.
40. Luis Farré, *Cincuenta años de filosofía en Argentina*, Buenos Aires, 1958, p. 80.

41. Ingenieros, *Proposiciones*, p. 44.
42. loc. cit.
43. op. cit., p. 32.
44. op. cit., p. 40.
45. Farré, op. cit., p. 74.
46. Ingenieros, *Proposiciones*, p. 26.
47. Ingenieros, *Principios de Psicología*, p. 372.
48. Ingenieros, *Proposiciones*, p. 84.
49. op. cit., pp. 85-86.
50. loc. cit.
51. Ingenieros, *Principios de Psicología*, pp. 372-373.
52. op. cit., p. 215.
53. Torchia-Estrada, op. cit., p. 229.
54. José Ingenieros, *Le Dantec, Biólogo y filósofo*, Buenos Aires, 1928, p. 11
55. op. cit., p. 48.
56. op. cit., p. 54.
57. op. cit., p. 55.
58. Ingenieros, *Le Dantec*, p. 68.
59. op. cit., p. 73.
60. op. cit., p. 75.
61. op. cit., p. 87.
62. op. cit., 108.
63. Héctor P. Agosti, op. cit. pp. 68-69.
64. op. cit., pp. 71-72.
64a. Aníbal Ponce, op. cit., pp. 33-34.
64b. op. cit., p. 36.
64c. op. cit., p. 37.
65. José Ingenieros, *La cultura filosófica en España*, 1916.
66. Ingenieros, *Proposiciones*, p. 25.
67. José Ingenieros, *Emilio Boutroux y la filosofía universitaria en Francia*, Buenos Aires, 1923, p. 25.
68. op. cit., p. 46.
69. op. cit., p. 60.
70. loc. cit.
71. loc. cit.
72. op. cit., pp. 61-62.
73. op. cit., pp. 85-86.
74. op. cit., p. 87.
75. op. cit., p. 144.
76. op. cit., p. 145.
77. op. cit., p. 151.
78. op. cit., p. 156.
79. José Ingenieros, *Hacia una moral sin dogmas*, Buenos Aires, 1947, 3rd ed., 1961, p. 22.
80. José Ingenieros, *Las fuerzas morales*, Buenos Aires, 1951, pp. 94-95.
81. op. cit., p. 32.
82. José Ingenieros, *El hombre mediocre*, Buenos Aires, 1961.
83. See also: José Ingenieros, *Los tiempos nuevos*, Buenos Aires, 1957.
84. Ingenieros, *El hombre mediocre*, p. 14.

85. op. cit., p. 22.
86. op. cit., p. 198.
87. Ingenieros, *Hacia una moral sin dogmas*, p. 105.
88. op. cit., p. 98.
89. op. cit., p. 16 ff.
90. op. cit., p. 23.
91. ibid, p. 171.

CHAPTER THREE

1. Francisco Aguilar, "Alejandro Korn, en el recuerdo", *Alejandro Korn, Homenaje en el centenario de su nacimiento,* Universidad del Litoral, Rosario, 1962, p. 16.
1a. Francisco Romero, *Alejandro Korn, Filósofo de la libertad,* Buenos Aires, 1956, p. 53.
1b. Alejandro Korn, *Obras,* Buenos Aires, 1949, p. 709.
1c. Raúl Alberto Pierola, "Alejandro Korn y el pensamiento argentino", *Cursos y Conferencias,* Buenos Aires, vols. 169-177, 1946, pp. 7-20.
2. Korn, *Obras,* pp. 211-212.
3. Francisco Romero, A. Vassallo and L. Aznar, *Alejandro Korn,* Buenos Aires, 1940, pp. 49-50.
4. Korn, *Obras,* p. 509.
5. loc. cit.
6. op. cit., p. 511.
7. Eugenio Pucciarelli, "Alejandro Korn y el pensamiento europeo", *Revista de la Universidad Nacional de La Plata,* no. 12, septiembre-diciembre de 1960, pp. 47-48.
8. Korn, *Obras,* p. 346.
9. op. cit., p. 347.
10. op. cit., p. 353.
11. op. cit., p. 354.
12. op. cit., 355.
13. op. cit., 359.
14. op. cit., 361.
14a. op. cit., 362.
15. op. cit., p. 76.
16. op. cit., p. 573.
17. See Chapter I.
18. Korn, *Obras,* p. 158.
19. op. cit., p. 161.
20. op. cit., p. 167.
21. Luis Romero, *Las ideas políticas en Argentina,* Buenos Aires, 1946. Chapter VII.
22. Korn, *Obras,* p. 172.
23. See Chapter I.
24. Korn, *Obras,* p. 178.
25. op. cit., p. 174.
26. See Chapter II.
27. Korn, *Obras,* p. 595.
28. op. cit., p. 599.

29. op. cit. p. 477.
30. See Ingenieros' discussion of Boutroux, Chapter II.
31. loc. cit. p. 477.
31a. op. cit. p. 478.
32. op. cit., p. 480.
33. op. cit., pp. 340-341.
34. F. Romero, A. Vasallo, and L. Aznar, op. cit., p. 70
35. Korn, *Obras,* p. 216.
36. op. cit., p. 217.
37. loc. cit.
38. op. cit., p. 213.
39. op. cit., p. 215.
40. op. cit., p. 220.
41. op. cit., pp. 303-304.
42. op. cit., p. 304.
43. op. cit., p 306.
44. op. cit., p. 309.
45. op. cit., p. 312.
46. loc. cit.
47. op. cit., p. 314.
48. op. cit., p. 316.
49. op. cit., p. 322.
50. op. cit., p. 242.
51. op. cit., p. 219.
52. loc. cit.
53. op. cit., p. 223.
54. loc. cit.
55. op. cit., p. 217.
56. loc. cit.
57. op. cit., p. 224.
58. loc. cit.
59. op. cit., p. 225.
60. Pucciarelli, op. cit., pp. 29-55.
61. op. cit., pp. 211-212.
62. op. cit., pp. 477-478.
63. op. cit., p. 341.
64. op. cit., p. 227.
65. op. cit., p. 229.
66. loc. cit.
67. op. cit., p. 295.
68. op. cit., p. 336.
69. op. cit., p. 338.
70. op. cit. pp. 339-340.
71. op. cit., p. 340.
72. op. cit., p. 271.
73. op. cit., p. 338.
74. Korn, *Obras,* p. 227.
75. César Barja, "Alejandro Korn," *Revista iberoamericana,* Vol. II núm. 4, noviembre de 1950, pp. 359-382.
76. Korn, *Obras,* pp. 288-289.

77. op. cit., pp. 291-292.
78. op. cit., p. 295.
79. Luis Farré, op. cit., p. 118.
80. W. J. Kilgore, "Alejandro Korn y la teoría relativista de los valores," *Philosophia*, Mendoza, Argentina, no. 23, 1959, p. 27.
81. Korn, *Obras*, p. 240.
82. loc. cit.
83. op. cit., p. 241.
84. op. cit., p. 323.
85. op. cit., p. 325.
86. op. cit., p. 327.
87. op. cit., p. 486.
88. op. cit., p. 485 ff.
89. op. cit., p. 487.
90. op. cit., p. 490.
91. op. cit., p. 476.
91a. op. cit., p. 384.
92. op. cit., p. 384.
93. op. cit., p. 385.
94. op. cit., p. 378.
95. Kilgore, op. cit., p. 60.
96. Korn, *Obras*, pp. 291-292.
97. W. J. Kilgore, "Estudios sobre Alejandro Korn," *Homenaje en el centenario de su nacimiento*, La Plata, 1963, p. 59.
98. op. cit., pp. 63-64.

CHAPTER FOUR

1. Rubén Sierra Mejía, "Francisco Romero," *Ideas y Valores*, Bogotá, vol. iv, no. 15-16, octubre de 1962—marzo de 1963, pp. 71-75.
2. op. cit., p. 73.
3. Francisco Romero, *Filosofía de la persona*, Buenos Aires, 1944.
4. Francisco Romero, *Teoría del hombre*, Buenos Aires, 1952.
5. F. Romero, *Filosofía de la persona* (2nd ed.) p. 9.
6. op. cit., p. 18.
6a. op. cit. pp. 19-20.
7. op. cit., p. 11.
8. op. cit., p. 35.
9. op. cit., p. 36.
10. Francisco Romero, *Filosofía contemporánea*, Buenos Aires, 1953.
11. op. cit., p. 165.
12. op. cit., p. 166.
13 op. cit., p. 168.
14. op. cit., p. 170.
15. Francisco Romero, *Papeles para una filosofía*, Buenos Aires, 1945, p. 13.
16. F. Romero, *Filosofía contemporánea*, p .170.
17. op. cit., p. 171.
18. op. cit., p. 172.
19. F. Romero, *Teoria del hombre*, 2nd ed., 1958, p. 169.

20. Francisco Romero, *Programa de una filosofía*, Buenos Aires, 1940.
21. *Teoría del hombre*, pp. 66-67.
22. Ibid., p. 77.
23. Ibid., p. 78.
24. Ibid., p. 18.
25. Ibid., p. 128.
26. loc. cit.
27. Ibid., p. 132.
28. Ibid., p. 146.
29. Ibid., p. 144.
30. Ibid., p. 153.
31. Ibid., p. 155.
32. Ibid., p. 161.
33. Ibid., 246.
34. Ibid., p. 251.
35. Ibid., p. 259.
36. Ibid., 264.
37. Ibid., p. 161.
38. Ibid., p. 165ff,
39. *Filosofía de la persona*, p. 55.
40. Ibid., p. 44.
41. Francisco Romero, *Filosofía de ayer y de hoy*, Madrid, 1960, p. 160.
42. L. Farré, op. cit., p. 173.
43. F. Romero, *Papeles para una filosofía*, p. 11.
44. Ibid., p. 12.
45. *Teoría del hombre*, p. 169.
46. *Papeles para una filosofía*, p. 14.
47. Hugo Rodríguez-Alcalá, *Misión y pensamiento de Francisco Romero*, México, 1959, p. 78.
48. *Teoría del hombre*, p. 171.
49. Ibid., p. 215.
50. Ibid., p. 172.
51. Ibid., pp. 176-177.
52. Ibid., p. 185.
53. Ibid., p. 214.
54. Ibid., p. 213.
55. Augusto Salazar Bondy, "Notas sobre las ideas axiológicas de Francisco Romero," *Homenaje a Francisco Romero*, Universidad de Buenos Aires, 1964, p. 170.
56. *Filosofía de la persona*, (1st ed., 1944), p. 11.
57. Francisco Romero, *El Hombre y la cultura*, Buenos Aires, 1950, pp. 9-16.
58. Ibid., p. 49.
59. Ibid., pp. 51-52.
60. Ibid., p. 60.
61. Ibid., p. 62.
62. Ibid., p. 63.
63. Ibid., p. 64.
64. *Papeles para una filosofía*, p. 124.
65. Ibid., p. 23.

66. *Filosofía contemporánea,* p. 60.
67. "En torno a la idea del progreso," *El Hombre y la cultura,* p. 65.
68. *Teoría del hombre,* pp. 93-116.
69. *El Hombre y la cultura,* p. 11.
70. *Teoría del hombre,* p. 96.
71. Ibid., p. 97.
72. Ibid., p. 113.
73. Ibid., p. 100.
74. Ibid., p. 58.
75. Ibid., p. 67.
76. Ibid., p. 105.
77. Risieri Frondizi, "La teoría del hombre de Francisco Romero," *Filosofía y Letras,* México, vol. xxv, núm. 49-50, enero-junio de 1953, p. 11.
78. *Teoría del hombre,* p. 194.
79. Ibid., p. 203.
80. Ibid., p. 204.
81. Ibid., p. 211 ff.
82. Ibid., p. 217.
83. Ibid., p. 220.
84. loc. cit.
85. Ibid., p. 224.
86. Ibid., p. 194.
87. Ibid., p. 227.
88. Ibid., 231.
89. Ibid., p. 186.
90. loc. cit.
91. Ibid., p. 187.
92. Francisco Romero, *Filósofos y problemas,* Buenos Aires, 1947, p. 148.
93. Ibid., p. 150.
94. Ibid., p. 151.
95. Ibid., pp. 156-157.
96. Francisco Romero, "Filosofía y libertad," *Asociación Argentina por la libertad de la cultura,* Buenos Aires, 1956, p. 35.
97. José Luis Romero, *Las ideas políticas en Argentina,* Buenos Aires, 1946, p. 229.
98. Francisco Romero, "Las alianzas de la filosofía", *La Torre,* Universidad de Puerto Rico, año II, núm. 6, junio de 1954.
99. "Filosofía y libertad," op. cit., p. 45.
100. Francisco Romero, "Reflexiones sobre la libertad política", *Ideas y figuras,* Buenos Aires, 1949, p. 127.
101. Francisco Romero, "La filosofía, la cultura y el hombre", *Filósofos y problemas,* Buenos Aires, 1947, p. 148.
102. Francisco Romero, *Sobre la filosofía en América,* Buenos Aires, 1952, p. 49.